CORNELL SCIENTIFIC INQUIRY SERIES

TEACHER'S GUIDE

Invasion
Ecology

NATIONAL SCIENCE TEACHERS ASSOCIATION

CORNELL SCIENTIFIC INQUIRY SERIES

TEACHER'S GUIDE

Invasion Ecology

BY THE ENVIRONMENTAL INQUIRY LEADERSHIP TEAM
MARIANNE KRASNY
NANCY TRAUTMANN
WILLIAM CARLSEN
CHRISTINE CUNNINGHAM

WITH CORNELL SCIENTIST DR. BERND BLOSSEY
ALAN FIERO (FARNSWORTH MIDDLE SCHOOL)
ADAM WELMAN

NATIONAL SCIENCE TEACHERS ASSOCIATION

NATIONAL SCIENCE TEACHERS ASSOCIATION

Claire Reinburg, Director
Judy Cusick, Associate Editor
Carol Duval, Associate Editor
Betty Smith, Associate Editor

ART AND DESIGN Linda Olliver, Director
   Cover image by Bernd Blossey, Cornell University
PRINTING AND PRODUCTION Catherine Lorrain-Hale, Director
   Nguyet Tran, Assistant Production Manager
   Jack Parker, Desktop Publishing Specialist
PUBLICATIONS OPERATIONS Erin Miller, Manager
MARKETING Holly Hemphill, Director
NSTA WEB Tim Weber, Webmaster
PERIODICALS PUBLISHING Shelley Carey, Director
sciLINKS Tyson Brown, Manager
NATIONAL SCIENCE TEACHERS ASSOCIATION
Gerald F. Wheeler, Executive Director
David Beacom, Publisher

Invasion Ecology
   NSTA Stock Number: PB162X4T
   ISBN: 0-87355-206-7
   Library of Congress Catalog Card Number: 98-84914
   Printed in the USA by Victor Graphics
   Printed on recycled paper

Library of Congress has catalogued the Student Edition as follows:
Invasion ecology / Marianne Krasny and the Environmental Inquiry Team— Student edition.
   p. cm. — (Cornell scientific inquiry series)
   ISBN 0-87355-211-3
   1. Biology invasions. I. Krasny, Marianne E. II. Series.
   QH353.I5835 2002
   577'.18—dc21   2002011620

NSTA is committed to publishing quality materials that promote the best in inquiry-based science education. However, conditions of actual use may vary and the safety procedures and practices described in this book are intended to serve only as a guide. Additional precautionary measures may be required. NSTA and the author(s) do not warrant or represent that the procedures and practices in this book meet any safety code or standard or federal, state, or local regulations. NSTA and the author(s) disclaim any liability for personal injury or damage to property arising out of or relating to the use of this book including any of the recommendations, instructions, or materials contained therein.

This material is based on the work supported by the National Science Foundation under Grant No. 96-18142. Any opinions, findings, conclusions or recommendations expressed in this material are those of the authors and do not necessarily reflect the views of the National Science Foundation.

Table of Contents
TEACHER'S GUIDE

Student Edition

ACKNOWLEDGMENTS

The Environmental Inquiry (EI) curriculum series represents a collaborative effort among scientists, science educators, Cornell students, and high school and middle school teachers. Without their input, these books could not have been produced. In particular, we wish to thank Dr. Bernd Blossey, assistant professor and director of the Biological Control of Invasive Plant Species Program at Cornell University. Dr. Blossey good-naturedly and enthusiastically mentored teachers as they worked to adapt the protocols he uses to study invasive species for use by secondary-level students. We think back fondly on Dr. Blossey's hearty laugh as he worked with those teachers and as he answered our questions about the science of biological control.

Farnsworth Middle School science teacher Alan Fiero worked with Dr. Blossey to adapt the purple loosestrife protocols for use with his students. Myndersee Academy biology teacher and Cornell graduate student Linda Tompkins, and Cornell students and National Science Foundation Graduate Teaching Fellows in K–12 Education (GK–12 fellows) Nancy Gift and Ben Wolfe, worked with Dr. Blossey to design the *Phragmites* research project for students. Without the enthusiasm of these and other EI teachers and students, this book would not have been possible.

Cornell scientist and educator Adam Welman worked tirelessly to check facts, test and write protocols, draft diagrams, and seek out illustrations. We thank him for being an integral partner in the latter, often hectic stages of putting the book together.

Teacher Alpa Kandhar and Cornell student Heather Clark adapted the soda lime protocol for use in classrooms. We also appreciate the efforts of Bill Brown and Nina Schoch from the Adirondack chapter of The Nature Conservancy in designing and piloting early detection surveys with volunteers. In addition, we would like to thank teachers and Cornell NSF GK–12 fellows Ty Atkins, Nicole Blenk, Virginia Collins, Anna Jensen, Aliya Haq, Sarah Lynne Reul, Angela Rivenshield, Jennifer Shirk, Rebecca Smyth, and Peter Weishampel for piloting activities and pointing out ways to enhance this book.

Ecologist Victoria Nuzzo served as a technical reviewer; we appreciate her careful attention to detail. Scientists Cliff Kraft, Kristi Sullivan, Rich Phillips, and Joseph Yavitt also helped to make sure the science was up-to-date and accurate. Suzanne Wapner and others in Professor Tim Fahey's lab provided space, materials, and equipment for testing protocols.

Leanne Avery has worked with us throughout the EI project. Formerly a high school science teacher and EI evaluator, currently a Ph.D. candidate and coordinator of our NSF GK–12 fellows program, she has spent countless hours in science classrooms observing teachers and GK–12 fellows. Her patient, thoughtful, and enthusiastic mentoring of teachers and Cornell fellows and her insights about how to improve EI have proved invaluable.

This book was reviewed by Michael J. Mappin, Program Coordinator, Environmental and Ecology Education Programs, University of Calgary, Calgary, Alberta; Joe Bradshaw, Science Teacher, Chief Joseph Middle School, Bozeman, Montana; and Barbara O'Neill, Science Department Chair, Mount Ararat High School, Topsham, Maine.

Invasion Ecology was produced by NSTA Press: Claire Reinburg, director; Carol Duval, project editor; Linda Olliver, art director; and Catherine Lorrain-Hale, production director.

Funding was provided by the National Science Foundation (NSF) Instructional Materials Development program. We thank our NSF program officers Trish Morse, David Campbell, and George DeBoer for helping us through the funding, writing, and production process. Additional support was provided by the NSF Graduate Teaching Fellows in K–12 Education program and by Cornell University.

Finally, we thank our families, including our parents, partners, and children, who provided understanding when we spent time away from them to work on the EI project.

INTRODUCTION

ENVIRONMENTAL INQUIRY

Invasion Ecology is part of the Environmental Inquiry (EI) curriculum series developed at Cornell University to enable high school students to conduct authentic environmental science research. The goals of EI are for students to

1. Develop research skills

2. Use their newly acquired skills to conduct environmental sciences research projects of their own design focusing on topics relevant to their local communities

3. Participate in communities of peer student scientists

4. Enhance their understanding of scientific content and process

Rather than learning science as a static body of facts, EI students experience the research process through which scientific understandings are formed and revised. Instead of memorizing a "scientific method," they discover for themselves the multifaceted nature of scientific research. And through studying problems relevant to their communities, they discover interconnections between science and society.

MEETING THE STANDARDS

The contemporary movement for science education reform calls for the teaching of science to reflect more closely the way in which science is practiced. According to the *National Science Education Standards* (National Research Council [NRC] 1996), the central strategy for teaching science should be to engage students in authentic inquiry or research.

> Students at all grade levels and in every domain of science should have the opportunity to use scientific inquiry and develop the ability to think and act in ways associated with the processes of inquiry, including asking questions, planning and conducting an investigation, using appropriate tools and techniques, thinking critically and logically about the relationships between evidence and explanations, constructing and analyzing alternative explanations, and communicating scientific arguments.
>
> (NRC 1996, 105)

The Science as Inquiry Standards call for all students to develop the following abilities:

▶ Identify questions and concepts that guide scientific investigations

▶ Design and conduct scientific investigations

▶ Use technology and mathematics to improve investigations and communications

▶ Formulate and revise scientific explanations and models using logic and evidence

▶ Recognize and analyze alternative explanations and models

▶ Communicate and defend a scientific argument
(NRC 1996, 175-6)

Using a stepwise approach, EI activities help students gain all these abilities as they design and carry out investigations and exchange ideas about their results with peer student scientists. A progression of worksheets guides students through each step of the inquiry process, providing structure but flexibility in designing and conducting meaningful projects. Students engaged in EI ecology research also will learn concepts and skills covered in other standards, including Science in Personal and Social Perspectives, History and Nature of Science, Life Science, and other areas. (See Table 1.)

WHY INQUIRY?

In addition to being integral to the *Standards*, understanding how scientists conduct research is essential for students as they become citizens capable of participating in a democracy. Like the general public, students often view science as a set of exercises with only one right answer. This leads to confusion when scientists publicly disagree about contentious issues such as global warming, food safety, or the impact of invasive species. How can both sides of the argument be right or scientific?

Once students have had the experience of carrying out their own research, they will understand better the challenges involved in addressing ecological questions and the reasons why scientists can't always come up with definitive answers. At the same time, they will understand that scientists work collaboratively, through a system called peer review, to ensure published results are the best answers they can find using present knowledge and technology. Students also will understand that, although science may not provide all the answers, it does provide a well-defined process for carrying out and reviewing research to reach the best explanations. Finally, because inquiry is both a social and creative process, it is an effective means of learning for students with a wide range of interests, learning styles, and achievement levels.

AUDIENCE

Invasion Ecology can be used as a module in biology, environmental science, ecology, botany, research, and general science courses, or as a resource for individual student research projects. In a growing number of schools, integrated science and environmental science are taught as introductory high school science courses. *Invasion Ecology* also works well in these classes because it does not assume detailed prior knowledge of the science disciplines and is based on thought-provoking hands-on activities.

The background text and research techniques in *Invasion Ecology* can be adapted for courses ranging from seventh grade through advanced placement science. Although research experiences commonly are reserved for advanced students, the EI curriculum series is designed to extend these opportunities to all students, including those who have not flourished in more traditional "college preparatory" science courses. EI pilot testing has shown that students who are not accustomed to thinking of themselves as scientists find motivation and self-esteem when faced with the challenge of carrying out authentic research projects and then reporting their results and exchanging constructive critiques with other students.

For more advanced science classes, *Invasion Ecology* provides opportunities to expand students' understanding of complex concepts related to ecology, invasive species, biological control, and the nature of conducting scientific research.

TABLE 1
National Science Education Standards Addressed through EI Research on Invasive Species Ecology

National Science Education Standards (NRC 1996)	Addressed in *Invasion Ecology*									
	Chapter 1 – Introduction	Chapter 2 – Population Ecology	Chapter 3 – Community Ecology	Chapter 4 – Ecosystem Ecology	Protocol 1 – Early Detection Surveys	Protocol 2 – Plot Sampling	Protocol 3 – Transect Surveys	Protocol 4 – Measuring Decomposition: Soda Lime	Protocol 5 – Measuring Decomposition: Titration	Interactive Research
Unifying Concepts and Processes in Science										
Systems, order, and organization	●	●	●	●	●	●	●	●		●
Evidence, models, and explanation	●	●	●	●	●	●	●	●	●	●
Change, constancy, and measurement	●	●	●	●	●	●	●	●	●	●
Evolution and equilibrium				●	●					
Science as Inquiry										
Abilities necessary to do scientific inquiry					●	●	●	●	●	●
Understandings about scientific inquiry	●	●	●	●	●	●	●	●	●	●
Physical Science										
Chemical reactions				●					●	
Life Science										
Biological evolution			●							
Interdependence of organisms	●	●	●	●	●	●	●	●	●	●
Matter, energy, and organization in living systems	●	●	●	●	●	●	●	●	●	●
Earth and Space Science										
Geochemical cycles				●						
Science and Technology										
Understandings about science and technology	●	●	●	●	●	●	●	●	●	●
Science in Personal and Social Perspectives										
Population growth	●	●								
Natural resources	●	●	●	●	●	●	●	●	●	●
Environmental quality	●	●	●	●	●	●	●	●	●	●
Natural and human-induced hazards	●	●	●	●	●	●	●	●	●	●
Science and technology in local, national, and global challenges	●	●	●	●	●	●	●	●	●	●
History and Nature of Science										
Science as a human endeavor	●	●	●	●	●	●	●	●	●	●
Nature of scientific knowledge	●	●	●	●	●	●	●	●	●	●
Historical perspectives	●	●	●							

WHY ECOLOGY OF INVASIVE SPECIES?

Ecology is a standard part of the life sciences curriculum. However, it is often only cursorily addressed. *Invasion Ecology* attempts to help students learn about this important scientific discipline in a rigorous manner and to apply ecological concepts to real-life environmental issues.

Your students may think of ecologists as people who pick up trash and protest for a cleaner environment. In this manual, we use the term ecologist to refer to scientists who study ecology—that is, the study of relationships among organisms and between organisms and their physical environment.

AUTHENTIC SCIENCE

Pick up any newspaper and you will be confronted with an array of environmental concerns ranging from global warming to local water supplies. Americans are concerned about the health of our environment, but we are uncertain how environmental issues should be taught in schools. Ecology, similarly to other sciences, sets forth fundamental principles that can be used to help us understand and manage our environment. Although no scientist can claim to be totally neutral, we can avoid more biased treatments of environmental issues by teaching students fundamental scientific principles and how to apply them toward solving environmental problems.

RELEVANCE

Invasive species constitute one of the most important threats to biodiversity in North America. Species are introduced, either accidentally or for a specific purpose, from every continent except Antarctica. About 1% of these species becomes invasive, outcompeting native plants and altering the habitat of native species. In agricultural lands, introduced invasive species cause millions of dollars in control measures and render some land unsuitable for cultivation. Along lake shores, zebra mussels can make it impossible to walk or swim in shallow areas. When species such as garlic mustard and purple loosestrife invade forests and wetlands, they outcompete native plant species, which in turn reduces the habitat and food available for wildlife. In cities, insects such as the Asian longhorned beetle kill ornamental trees treasured by communities, whereas the Norwegian rat, introduced several hundred years ago, may cause human health problems.

In today's global economy, with cut flowers flown in daily from Europe and South America and people flying back and forth between continents, we are not able to close our borders entirely and prevent all new species from entering North America. We may be able to take some measures to limit the introduction of new species, such as treating ballast waters in ships and conducting awareness campaigns. For species that still enter accidentally or that are already established, we can use ecological science to develop effective means of control. Learning about ecology and invasive species allows students to address problems relevant to many different communities throughout North America.

ENGAGING STUDENTS

Some ecology courses teach ecological principles and then give a variety of examples. We have taken a slightly different approach—starting with real-life examples of the history and impact of invasive species and then using the examples to teach ecological concepts and principles. In addition, we present opportunities for students to engage in hands-on research, modeled after that conducted by scientists studying invasive species and other ecological problems. Thus, students learn about one discipline and one major environmental issue in depth, as well as principles and methods that can be applied to studying other ecological problems. By presenting the information in this way, we hope to engage students more fully in studying ecological science.

In sum, through the readings, exercises, protocols, and research projects in *Invasion Ecology*, students will learn not only about important ecological concepts, but also about how ecologists conduct research. Furthermore, they will learn how ecological science and research can be applied to solving a real-life environmental problem—the control of invasive species.

INQUIRY AND ECOLOGY

LEVELS OF INQUIRY

Environmental science is organized into two levels of inquiry modeled after research activities conducted by professional scientists. In general, when novice scientists first enter a lab, they learn a series of techniques from the more experienced scientists. Once they have mastered these techniques, they are encouraged to develop their own, open-ended research projects. Throughout this process, they interact with their peer scientists, who help them sharpen their research skills.

Similarly, in Environmental Inquiry (EI), students first learn standard research methods, or *protocols*. EI protocols introduce students to laboratory and field methods adapted from university research so they are feasible and safe for use by high school students. The protocols are inexpensive to carry out, yet are authentic techniques used by professional scientists. Experience with the protocols helps students develop basic skills and understandings they will be able to use in designing and carrying out more open-ended scientific investigations.

Having mastered one or more protocols, students are likely to come up with questions that could be addressed through open-ended, or interactive, research. This level is called *interactive research* rather than simply research because it emphasizes working collaboratively, similar to the way scientists work with their peers in laboratories and field settings.

Interactive research is designed for students to follow the steps scientists normally conduct, including

▶ Narrowing down an interesting research question

▶ Using appropriate protocols to answer their question

▶ Sharing observations and advice with students conducting similar studies

▶ Discussing various possible interpretations of research results

▶ Presenting findings in oral or written form

▶ Participating in peer review of research presentations

▶ Recommending ideas and approaches for future research

As EI students move from protocols to interactive research, they accept increasing levels of responsibility for the design of their investigations. Similarly, there is a progression in interaction among students as they work with peers to define questions, analyze their results, argue among alternative interpretations, and communicate their findings to fellow student scientists and community members (see Figure 1).

FIGURE 1
Levels of Inquiry in EI

Protocols
Standard exercises where students learn skills and develop understandings. Students work together to plan their protocols and review their results.

Develop a question for investigation using one or more protocols.

Interactive Research
Investigations where students work collaboratively with peers to develop a valid question, plan methods, and analyze, interpret, and present results.

If possible, design new research projects, revising the research question and/or the approach based on previous results.

COOPERATION AND PEER REVIEW IN SCIENCE

A common misconception among students is that scientists are social loners who work in isolation with little connection to each other or society. In fact, research is a cumulative process, with each scientist learning from the work of preceding and contemporary researchers. Before embarking on a research endeavor, scientists typically begin by talking with colleagues, listening to presentations at conferences, and reading publications to learn what has already been accomplished and what questions remain unanswered.

Although much of the interaction among scientists is informal, researchers also have devised a formal process, called peer review, to help them separate fact from falsehood and good science from bad. Peer review, in which scientists critically review the research of another scientist working in the same field, plays a key role in determining which research endeavors receive funding, which conference papers get accepted, and which articles get published in journals. Just as importantly, the constructive comments provided by peer reviewers help scientists improve their research projects.

Thus, scientists depend on discussions with their peers to help them narrow down research questions, determine which methods are most appropriate to address those questions, and make sure the interpretations of their results are valid. In EI, we have attempted to reproduce such collaborations for students, both face-to-face and electronically with their peers in other classes and schools. Through modeling collaborative processes that are integral to professional scientific communities, EI students improve their own work and enhance their critical-thinking skills. In addition, we have found that by participating in science as a social rather than an individualistic endeavor, students who tend to shy away from science may find it fun and so become engaged.

ECOLOGICAL RESEARCH

Although many people may think research always involves a controlled experiment, ecological research takes on a variety of forms. Nearly all ecological research involves careful fieldwork (work outdoors). Ecologists working in a new area may start by making an inventory of the plant and animal species. Once they have an idea of what is present, they often monitor changes in populations of organisms and in physical factors without imposing any experimental treatment. They may establish permanent plots so they can monitor species over a period of time. In fact, many ecological questions can be answered only by long-term studies (e.g., the response of a forest to clear-cutting or fire).

Once they are familiar with the species and physical factors at their research sites, ecologists may conduct a "natural" experiment in which they compare species in two or more habitats. For example, after observing that frog populations were declining in agricultural areas, scientists measured pollution levels and the health of frog populations in a series of lakes varying in exposure to agricultural chemicals. They then tried to correlate frog health to pollution levels. Although such a natural experiment may provide important evidence, it is not a true controlled experiment because the lakes vary in a number of ways, in addition to their exposure to agricultural chemicals. Furthermore, it is difficult to determine whether any differences in frog populations are due to differences in pollution in the lakes or to some other factor such as disease or the ability of certain types of frogs to colonize the different lakes.

In fact, scientists only rarely are able to conduct a true controlled experiment in the field, because study sites generally differ (e.g., in soil nutrients, slope, plant species), and thus they cannot find good controls. Nevertheless, some ecologists do impose treatments and compare treatment sites to reference sites, which are as similar as possible to the treatment sites. A famous example of such a "field experiment" in ecology occurred at the Hubbard Brook Experimental Forest in New Hampshire, where scientists clear-cut an entire watershed and compared the regrowth of plants there to growth in a watershed that had not been cut.

Laboratory studies offer ecologists a chance to study processes that occur in the field under more controlled conditions. For example, Cornell scientists measured methane production in outdoor wetlands. In a related laboratory study, they used measured methane production in quart mason jars of various soils gathered from the wetlands. In the laboratory study, the scientists were able to vary temperature while controlling for other factors such as soil type. Thus, such a laboratory study can determine the relationship of temperature to methane production under controlled conditions. However, ecologists still need to conduct fieldwork to determine whether what happens in the laboratory really represents what occurs under natural conditions, where many factors in addition to temperature interact.

In short, it generally is not possible to conduct one study to definitively answer an ecological question. Rather, ecologists answer questions by using a variety of approaches at different scales, ranging from broad field surveys to controlled laboratory studies. They then piece together the evidence from these different investigations to determine the best possible answer to their question.

TABLE 2
Intended Learning Outcomes

Skills: Students will be able to

▶ Conduct scientific research, starting with well-defined protocols and progressing to open-ended research projects

▶ Work collaboratively to design research projects, interpret results, and critically analyze ideas and conclusions

▶ Define a research question, then plan and carry out a study to address this question using surveys or other types of studies

▶ Analyze data and draw conclusions about invasive species

▶ Write a concise and accurate summary of methods, results, and conclusions

▶ Use commentary from fellow students to revise or justify research reports and presentations

▶ Critically analyze summaries of other students' research to determine whether each study was based on good research design

▶ Provide constructive criticism of fellow students' data analyses, interpretations, and conclusions

Concepts: Students will understand that

▶ Ecology is the study of living things and their interactions with each other and the physical environment

▶ Population ecology is the study of how populations of organisms change in size and location

▶ Community ecology is the study of how organisms interact with each other and how groups of organisms change over time

▶ Ecosystem ecology is the study of how organisms interact with the physical environment

▶ Invasive species are an important threat to biodiversity in North America

▶ Biological control is one of several alternatives to controlling invasive species

▶ Monitoring, laboratory, and field studies all contribute to our understanding of ecological systems

▶ Scientists work both individually and collaboratively, reviewing each other's work to provide feedback on experimental design and interpretation of results; these "peer reviews" are used to make decisions about what research gets funded and what results get published in scientific journals

▶ Scientific understandings are tentative, subject to change with new discoveries; peer review among scientists helps sort genuine discoveries from incomplete or faulty work

GUIDING STUDENT INQUIRY

ABOUT THE STUDENT EDITION

Through the *Invasion Ecology* Teacher's Guide and Student Edition, we have tried to provide information and suggestions to help teachers guide students in inquiry-based science. This chapter includes information to help teachers guide students through the background text, protocols, and interactive research projects, which make up the three main sections of the Student Edition. At the end of the chapter, we provide teaching tips for guiding students in developing research skills and eventually in conducting their own research projects.

Section 1—Understanding Invasion Ecology

Four chapters of background text covering basic ecological concepts and principles. Each chapter concludes with a series of discussion questions, which encourage critical thinking about the chapter content and about how one might conduct research related to the ecological concepts covered. Several chapters also include exercises to prepare students to conduct protocols.

Section 2—Invasion Ecology Protocols: Introducing Research

Five protocols providing specific instruction on ecological research techniques.

Section 3—Beyond Protocols: Conducting Interactive Research

Suggestions for developing interactive research projects using these protocols. Included are two example interactive research projects that students are conducting in cooperation with Cornell scientists.

Forms designed to help students carry out protocols and interactive research are included in Sections 1 and 2.

UNDERSTANDING INVASION ECOLOGY

The first chapter of the Student Edition provides an introduction to invasive species and ecology. Each of the three remaining chapters emphasizes one of the three main branches of ecology: population, community, and ecosystem. Extensive, real-life examples of how ecological concepts and principles can be applied to problems with invasive species are included in each chapter. You will find sidebars at appropriate points throughout the background text that provide short explanations of nature of science concepts, such as disagreement among scientists and uncertainty in science.

At the end of each chapter are discussion questions. Note that many of the questions involve drawing a diagram or graph. We have found that asking students to draw on the board helps stimulate discussion. We have included model responses to these questions below.

MODEL RESPONSES TO DISCUSSION QUESTIONS

Chapter 1. Introduction

▶ What are some invasive species in your area?

Many excellent websites about invasive species are accessible through SciLinks. Look for sites from environmental organizations such as The Nature Conservancy, state and federal natural resources and conservation agencies, and universities to find local species of concern.

▶ What are some of the problems invasive species are causing in your area or elsewhere?

Animal invaders can prey on or compete with native wildlife and feed on native plants, thus reducing biodiversity. Plant invaders can compete with native plants, thus reducing biodiversity. Plant and some animal invaders, including tamarisk, zebra mussels, and earthworms, may alter hydrologic regimes, water quality, and carbon and nutrient cycles, thus altering ecosystems and negatively impacting native species. Microorganisms may cause diseases (e.g., the chestnut blight) that reduce or decimate populations of native species. Invasive species also may become serious insect and weed problems in agriculture.

▶ Why do humans value biodiversity?

Humans value biodiversity for abstract—aesthetic, ethical, and spiritual—and practical reasons. Some people enjoy observing organisms or simply knowing they exist. Others value species for their potential benefits to humans, such as foods and medicines. Scientists believe we are currently losing biodiversity at an unprecedented rate. The impacts of such losses are not completely understood but will be very serious.

▶ A number of wildlife species that were once rare are making a comeback. For example, finding groups of up to six white-tailed deer in the middle of suburban yards in Ithaca, New York, is not uncommon. Elk are commonplace and can be seen downtown in smaller cities, such as Banff, in the Rocky Mountains. Coyotes are known to eat pet cats in Portland, Oregon, and other western cities. And mountain lions are a concern to suburban communities in South Dakota, Colorado, and elsewhere. Why might some of these native animals be invading "human territory?" Which is the problem—the wildlife or the humans?

Wildlife species are making a comeback because of (1) a reduction in hunting pressure (reduced predation) and (2) an increase in suitable habitat (e.g., regrowth of forests). In some cases, government management strategies designed to increase populations of species once threatened by very low numbers have been successful. In the case of white-tailed deer, these strategies included controls on hunting and encouraging landowners to manage their land for mixed woods/open habitat, providing both protection from predators and preferred food plants.

Chapter 2. Population Ecology

▶ You are working for the U.S. Department of Agriculture and get a request from a nursery company to bring a new species into the U.S. for use as an ornamental plant. What questions might you ask about this species if you wanted to determine whether it was likely to become invasive?

Although scientists are not able to predict whether any one introduced plant will become invasive, the three characteristics of plants most strongly associated with invasiveness are species that (1) are native to climatic zones similar to those in North America, (2) have become invasive when introduced elsewhere, and (3) are established in gardens or agriculture (rather than as house plants). Other features associated with invasiveness include plants that (1) do not have predators (including herbivores) in North America, (2) grow rapidly so they are strong competitors with other plants or animals, (3) produce large numbers of seeds at a young age, (4) have seeds that can survive a long time before germinating, and (5) have seeds that spread over long distances.

▶ You have just discovered a small patch of the invasive plant garlic mustard in a local forest. Assuming nothing is done to control the garlic mustard, draw a diagram of the population curve you might expect for garlic mustard in this forest over the next five years. Now draw a curve for the next thirty years assuming no control measures are taken. Again assuming nothing is done to control the garlic mustard, draw population curves for the next five and next thirty years for native species that are already in the forest, such as trilliums, jack-in-the-pulpit, toothwort, and spring beauty.

Over the short term, we would expect an exponential growth curve. Eventually, the garlic mustard population will be limited by lack of space, nutrients, or some other factor, and we would expect the growth curve to be logistic. Species present when garlic mustard invades might show declining populations. They would not be expected to recover unless control measures were implemented.

▶ You and your classmates are conducting a survey to find out the distribution of a non-native, invasive plant that colonizes wetlands and has just entered your county. Draw a diagram or map of what you would expect its distribution to be. Now, assume the species has been in your county for twenty years, and no one has tried to control it. How does its distribution differ from when it first entered the county? Draw a map of how you think the plant would be distributed in the county if no control measures were taken. How would its distribution be different if control measures had been taken when it first entered the county?

An invasive species that has just begun to colonize a region would have very spotty distribution—likely a few small patches in one or more areas of suitable habitat. If control measures were taken, the populations may remain small and spotty. If no control measures were taken, we would expect the plant to colonize many suitable habitats in the county within a relatively short time.

Chapter 3: Community Ecology

▶ There has been a heated debate among ecologists about biological control. Some think it is wrong to introduce a new species to control a previously introduced species that has become invasive. They fear the control species may itself become invasive and cause more problems than the species it was introduced to control. To support this point of view, these scientists cite examples of where biological control has failed. Other scientists say that, with the safeguards now required in biological control programs, it is extremely unlikely an insect or other species introduced to control an invasive species will cause a problem. These scientists say we need to weigh this very tiny risk of a problem against the benefits of controlling unwanted invasive species.

What do you think are the pros and cons of using biological control for invasive species? How does biological control compare with other possible management options (e.g., applying herbicides, pulling up plants by hand, or burning)?

Every method of controlling unwanted species has advantages and disadvantages.

***Biological control.** It takes about ten years to conduct research to develop a biological control program. The program is specific for targeted species and does not impact nontarget species. When proper procedures are followed, there have been no known instances of introduced biocontrol species having negative impacts on nontarget species. The chance of species evolving to attack other species is very small. Species are introduced one time and reproduce on their own, so repeated control measures are not necessary.*

***Herbicides.** They may impact nontarget species. Some herbicides may have negative health effects on humans. Herbicides need to be applied repeatedly.*

***Pulling up plants.** The process is specific for target species, but may require digging out entire root systems. It is likely to need to be repeated every several years and it is labor intensive. It may cause additional disturbance to the soil, creating bare spots where seeds of invasive species are likely to germinate. Also, when a lot of people pull up plants, they trample down other vegetation. Pulling works best for small isolated clumps or initial small infestations.*

Burning. *Burning may impact nontarget species. It causes air pollution and likely needs to be combined with other control methods.*

▶ Learn about an invasive species following the directions for the **Invasive Species Profile** exercise below. Then discuss with your classmates the following questions about the species you have investigated.

    a. How have invasive species impacted food webs? Diagram the food web of the communities that have been invaded by the species you investigated, both before and after the species invaded.

    Invasive species may be more effective predators or herbivores than native species, in some cases replacing them in the food web. For example, the opossum shrimp is a more effective predator of phytoplankton than is salmon and thus negatively impacts salmon populations as well as the eagles and bears that prey on salmon. An invasive plant species may be less suitable as food for herbivores and thus cause declines in populations of herbivores and the predators that depend on them.

    b. List the habitats along with the invasive species present in each. What types of habitats appear to be vulnerable to invasive species?

    Disturbed and early successional habitats are most susceptible to invasive species, but they occur in all habitats including wetlands, lakes, grasslands, forests, oceans, and farm fields.

    c. Do the communities where invasive species are found tend to be early or late successional communities? What kinds of disturbances, in addition to invasive species, have impacted these communities?

    Although invasive species are more likely to be present in early successional communities, they can occur in late successional communities. Other disturbances include repeated mowing, commercial and residential development, fire, tornadoes and hurricanes, and forest cutting.

Chapter 4. Ecosystem Ecology

▶ Refer to the invasive species profiles you developed in Chapter 3 to answer the questions below. While discussing the questions, record any new questions you are not able to answer.

    a. Do any of the species you profiled have impacts on primary productivity? If so, what are they? Diagram the trophic levels or carbon cycle prior to the introduction of the invasive species. Then show on the diagram how the species impacts trophic relationships and the carbon cycle.

    Invasive species may impact the carbon cycle by changing rates of decomposition or by reducing populations of primary producers through competition and feeding on plants.

    b. Did anyone in your group find a species that impacts nitrogen or other nutrient cycles in the ecosystems in which it is found? If so, how would you describe these impacts? Draw a diagram of the nutrient cycle and show how the species is changing it.

Through changing decomposition rates, invasive species may change the nitrogen cycle. For example, increased decomposition rates may lead to more nitrogen leaching into ground and surface water, causing water contamination and eutrophication. Increased decomposition rates also may reduce the amount of nitrogen available to plants.

c. Did anyone in your group find a species that impacts water dynamics? If so, draw a diagram to show how water dynamics have changed as a result of the species.

Invasive species may be more effective than native species at taking up water from the soil and thus may create water shortages for native species and irrigation, or increase fire hazards.

▶ As you were trying to answer the questions above, you likely were confronted with some new questions you couldn't answer. The answers to some of these questions may not be known. Outline a research project to answer one of these questions. Will your research include observations, experiments outdoors, and/or experiments in the lab or greenhouse?

Often a combination of research methods is needed to answer an ecological question focusing on invasive species or other phenomena. For example, scientists may first monitor what species are in the area, next impose control measures and evaluate their effectiveness using plot sampling, and also determine their impacts on ecosystems using outdoor or microcosm experiments.

▶ You have read about two types of impacts on aquatic ecosystems: eutrophication caused by excess phosphorus and changes in biodiversity and water clarity caused by zebra mussels. How might eutrophication be reduced? How might populations of zebra mussels be reduced? Is there a difference in our ability to control chemical pollution and "biological pollution"?

Eutrophication can be controlled by reducing phosphorus inputs through changing agricultural practices (e.g., fertilizer and manure applications). We do not currently have any good methods for controlling zebra mussels in lakes other than preventing their introduction to new sites by carefully cleaning boats after they have been in a lake with zebra mussels. Where zebra mussels coat intake pipes on power plants, they can be removed mechanically.

INVASION ECOLOGY PROTOCOLS—
INTRODUCING RESEARCH

OVERVIEW: PROTOCOLS AND FORMS

Protocols are techniques or methods scientists use in their research. It is important to understand the protocols and, in many cases, to practice them before embarking on an independent research project. Although we have provided example research projects in Section 3, students also can design their own research projects using the protocols in this section.

Protocols 1 through 3 involve *fieldwork*, or work outdoors. They provide information useful in making decisions about control of invasive species. For example, the land manager at a state park needs information about what new problem species are invading the park, what invasive species already are present, how large their populations are, and the effectiveness of control measures such as herbicides or biological control.

Protocols 4 and 5 are *microcosm* experiments—they examine processes that occur in nature using soil samples in a small container. In Chapter 3 of the Student Edition, we described microcosm experiments used to study competition between two different aquatic microorganisms. In the microcosm protocols in this manual, students will measure decomposition in soil samples placed in airtight, shallow plastic containers. In microcosm experiments, students can control factors, such as temperature, that they are not able to control outdoors.

Safety is a concern for all field and lab work. If students are working where there are tall plants such as purple loosestrife and *Phragmites,* they should wear eye protection to avoid getting poked in the eye. Goggles and gloves should be worn for the microcosm protocols, which involve handling potentially harmful chemicals.

Three types of worksheets are included with the protocols. Although the purpose of conducting protocols is to learn a specific technique enabling students to carry out an independent research project, students still should recognize that each protocol is

TABLE 3
Steps in Carrying Out an EI Protocol

Activity	Collaborative and Individual Work	Peer Review Process
Planning to use a protocol	Students work individually or collaboratively to fill the **Protocol Planning Form** (p. 116).	N.A.
Carrying out a protocol	Students work in groups to conduct a protocol.	N.A.
Analyzing and presenting the results	Students work individually or collaboratively to report and analyze data using one of the **Data Forms** for each protocol. Students then write individual lab reports.	Before students write their reports, groups pair up to discuss and compare results using the **Data Analysis Peer Review Form** (p. 118).

designed to address a specific question. The **Protocol Planning Form** should help students make the connection between the question they are addressing and the technique they are learning. **Data Forms** guide students through the appropriate steps in data collection, analysis, and interpretation, including the final step of generating ideas for follow-up, open-ended research. To emphasize that collaborative work is integral to EI, including at the protocol level, students who have completed a protocol can provide constructive feedback on each other's results and conclusions and exchange written feedback using the **Data Analysis Peer Review Form**. This step introduces students to the benefits of exchanging constructive criticism, both to sharpen their own thinking and to provide advice to their peers.

Protocol 1. Early Detection Surveys is a survey of an area, such as a park or nature preserve, for any problem species that might be in the process of invading. For managers wanting to control invasive species, it is important to know which species are starting to invade, because the most effective management strategy is to control small patches of invasive species before they spread.

Protocol 2. Plot Sampling—Density and Percent Cover provides an estimate of how common invasive and other species are. Plot Sampling—Density involves counting the stems of species within a small area (often 1 m^2) called a plot or quadrat. Plot Sampling—Percent Cover involves estimating the percent of the space a species covers in a plot. These measures can be repeated to show changes in populations of invasive and other species over time. They also can be used to compare plant populations in different habitats or before and after different management treatments (e.g., releasing biological control insects). Before students carry out the plot survey protocol, they will learn how to locate plots using random or stratified sampling methods. By using random or stratified sampling to locate plots, they will avoid choosing plots that are close or easy to sample, which would bias their results. Students also need to construct quadrat frames using PVC tubing or meter sticks prior to plot sampling.

Protocol 3. Transect Surveys involves sampling plants along a line or transect. Transect surveys can be used to determine differences in plant populations as you move from one habitat to another. For example, transect surveys could be used if you wanted to know whether the population of an invasive species changed as you moved from a disturbed roadside to an undisturbed forest. They also can be used to survey along trails, which are often the sites where invasive species are first found.

Protocol 4. Measuring Decomposition Using Soda Lime is unlike the first three protocols in that it does not involve measuring plant populations in the field. Instead, this protocol measures the rate of decomposition in a sample of organic material or soil. The amount of CO_2 produced by the sample is used to estimate the rate of decomposition. This is because the microorganisms that decompose organic matter in soil produce CO_2 and thus, the more CO_2 produced, the higher the rate of decomposition.

The method used in Protocol 4 involves weighing the amount of CO_2 absorbed by a small amount of soda lime in a container with the organic material or soil sample. It requires a balance sensitive to 0.01 g. If students have access to this type of balance in the classroom, the protocol can be used as written. If students do not have access to a precise balance, but teachers do (e.g., in the chemistry lab), the protocol still can be conducted. In this case, teachers will need to weigh and dry the soda lime before and after the incubation, but the students can carry out the rest of the protocol. Note that the success of this protocol depends on very accurate, consistent weighing techniques. Furthermore, a more precise balance (e.g., one that can measure to 0.001 or 0.0001 grams) will yield even better results. Before conducting the soda lime protocol, students will need to obtain samples of soils in the field and measure their moisture content.

Protocol 5. Measuring Decomposition Using a Titration is similar to Protocol 4 in that it measures CO_2 produced by a soil or organic material sample. However, in this protocol, the CO_2 is trapped by a sodium hydroxide solution rather than by soda lime in the form of pellets. Protocol 5 uses a titration rather than a change in weight to measure the amount of CO_2 produced by the soil or organic material sample. Students should be familiar with titrations before embarking on this protocol. This method is slightly more complicated than the soda lime protocol but has the added benefit of teaching students important laboratory skills and more chemistry. Before conducting the titration protocol, students will need to obtain samples of soils in the field and measure their moisture content.

We suggest using shallow, airtight plastic containers to incubate soils for Protocols 4 and 5. For the titration protocol, you could use other types of airtight containers such as gallon jars, but the soda lime requires a flat container to spread out the soil. This is because soda lime is less efficient than NaOH at absorbing CO_2, and thus you need a larger soil surface area to get results.

USING THE PROTOCOLS IN RESEARCH

Early detection surveys can be used to answer questions that population ecologists might ask, such as what are the abundance and distribution of an invasive species. Plot sampling and transect surveys provide more information about the abundance of species and they also can be used to answer questions in community ecology, such as how plant communities change over time. The two measuring decomposition protocols are used to answer questions related to carbon cycles, which are important to ecosystem ecologists.

Although the focus of this text is invasive species, many of the ecological questions we address also apply to other species. Thus, the plant protocols can be used to answer questions having to do with plants that aren't invasive, and the soils protocols can be used to answer questions about soils that don't have invasive species. Table 4 summarizes the different protocols.

Before embarking on a research project, scientists generally search the library and the Internet to find out what other scientists already have learned about their research topic. Students should familiarize themselves with the invasive species in their area, including what habitats they likely to be found in, how to identify them, and what some of the methods used to control them are before conducting Protocols 1 through 3 (See the **Invasive Species Profile** exercise, Chapter 3, p. 40). They might want to learn about soils in their area before conducting Protocols 4 and 5.

TABLE 4
Invasion Ecology Protocols

Question	Protocol	Examples
What invasive species currently are coming into a local area? How widespread are they and what habitats are they invading?	Early detection surveys	Volunteers conducted a survey along the trails at a local nature center. Foresters in Chicago and New York City conducted extensive surveys of street trees to determine if the Asian longhorned beetle was present.
Are our efforts to control species x having any effect? Is the population of species x changing over time? Does the population of species x differ in different habitats?	Plot sampling —Density (useful when the number of stems is easy to count) —Percent cover (useful when there are many small stems)	Scientists and students conducted plot surveys of purple loosestrife before and after releasing beetles used in biological control.
Are there any changes in what species are present as we move from one habitat to another?	Transect surveys	Garlic mustard may first invade a disturbed site along a roadside and then colonize the adjacent forest. Scientists and students could conduct a survey along a transect extending from the road into the forest.
Are invasive species changing the way carbon is cycling through the ecosystem?	Measuring decomposition	Scientists and high school students conducted a study of decomposition of soils and organic material with and without non-native worms.

FIGURE 2
Relationships among the Invasion Ecology Protocols

Classes can progress from one group of protocols to another or they can choose specific protocols of interest.

Area-Wide Surveys

Protocol 1. Early Detection Surveys

Early detection surveys can help locate a specific invasive species or habitat for further investigation using plot and transect surveys.

Plot and Transect Surveys

Protocol 2. Plot Sampling—Density and Percent Cover

Protocol 3. Transect Surveys

After learning about the plants on their plots, students may become interested in ecosystem processes. They can conduct Protocol 4 or 5 to learn about decomposition at their sites.

Decomposition Using Microcosms

Protocol 4. Measuring Decomposition Using Soda Lime

Protocol 5. Measuring Decomposition Using a Titration

BEYOND PROTOCOLS—
CONDUCTING INTERACTIVE RESEARCH

STEPS IN CONDUCTING INTERACTIVE RESEARCH

Once they have mastered the content and protocols, students are ready to engage in interactive research projects. Students conducting interactive research will

- Develop research questions

- Plan and carry out investigations using protocols

- Analyze, interpret, and report their results

- Conduct peer review of each other's work

- Respond to peer reviews of their own work

The EI student worksheets will help focus student attention on the important questions at each stage of the interactive research process. These forms are also available through the EI website *http://ei.cornell.edu* so you can adapt them to fit your specific classroom needs.

- **Choosing a Research Topic** (p. 160) guides students through the process of choosing a research question that is both feasible and interesting.

- **Interactive Research Planning Form 1** (p. 163) helps in planning the logistics of research.

- **Interactive Research Planning Form 2** (p. 165) serves the same role for experiments.

- **Research Report Form** (p. 170) guides students through the essentials of writing a research report, including a section on how they responded to peer reviews.

- **Poster Design Guidelines** (p. 173) outline how to put together a research poster.

- **Research Design Peer Review Form** (p. 174) provides students with guidelines for helping fellow students design research projects.

- **Research Report Peer Review Form** (p. 175) provides guidelines for students reviewing each other's reports.

- **Poster Peer Review Form** (p. 176) provides guidelines for students reviewing each other's posters.

TABLE 5
Steps in Interactive Research

Activity	Collaborative Work	Peer Review
Planning an experiment	Students work together to brainstorm research ideas, then fill out **Choosing a Research Topic** (p. 160) and **Interactive Research Planning Form 1** or **2** (pp. 163–169).	Student groups are paired up to discuss and refine research plans using the **Research Design Peer Review Form** (p. 174).
Carrying out the research	Students work in groups to conduct research.	N.A.
Analyzing and presenting the results	Students collaborate to analyze their data, then write research reports using the **Research Report Form** (p. 170) or create posters using the **Poster Design Guidelines** (p. 173).	Students present their research results and then exchange feedback using the **Research Report Peer Review Form** (p. 175) or **Poster Peer Review Form** (p. 176). Final reports incorporate changes generated through peer review.

EXAMPLE INTERACTIVE RESEARCH PROJECTS

Instructions and data forms for the following two interactive research projects are included in Section 3 of the Student Edition.

Example Interactive Research Project 1— Biological Control of Purple Loosestrife

Students raise and release beetles used in the biological control of purple loosestrife and then monitor their effect on populations of this significant wetland invasive species. This is a long-term project, involving surveying purple loosestrife populations in the fall, raising the beetles in the spring, and releasing them in late spring. Ideally, classes at your school will continue this project over a number of years so they can track the impact of their beetle releases on purple loosestrife populations.

Example Interactive Research Project 2— *Phragmites* Insect Survey

Students survey insect larvae on *Phragmites* (common reed) stems. Using the EI website, the results of student projects are shared online with Cornell scientists who are looking for insects that could be used in biological control of this invasive wetland species. This is a relatively short-term project for any one classroom. It involves collecting *Phragmites* stems and then having students or groups of students search for and identify insect larvae in the stems.

IDEAS FOR INTERACTIVE RESEARCH PROJECTS

Your students may want to choose their own research projects. Thus, we also have included some suggested research topics related to the protocols. Because all the protocols except for early detection surveys can be used to answer any number of ecological questions, we include suggestions for interactive research related to invasive species and other issues.

Long-term monitoring of new problem species invading a watershed, park, or preserve

Classes develop long-term monitoring projects to determine changes in invasive species present and in the approximate area they occupy within a watershed, park, or preserve. Because new species are continually being introduced to North America, classes can repeat these surveys from year to year. Archiving the results will allow students to compare how the species invading their area have changed over time.

Long-term monitoring of species present in the schoolyard

If there is an area of your schoolyard that is not landscaped, students can do annual surveys to follow changes in species composition over the years.

Changes in species composition following control measures for invasive species (e.g., burning, applying herbicides, pulling up plants, biological control)

There may be some sites in your community where government agencies or conservationists (e.g., land trusts) are attempting to control invasive species. Your students might embark on a community service project in cooperation with land managers to help control an invasive species. By setting up permanent plots on the site, students can help the land managers determine the results of their control strategies.

Comparison of species composition at sites where control measures have been taken and at sites left alone

Students working with land managers to evaluate the effectiveness of control measures may want to compare species composition at the site where control measures were taken and at a site that was left alone. They should try to choose sites as similar as possible and, if possible, to take measurements before and after control measures are implemented.

Comparison of species composition in sites where deer are excluded by a fence and in sites left alone

Some county Cooperative Extension offices, university field stations, and nature preserves may want to set up demonstration sites to show the effect of deer browse on tree regeneration. Students can conduct surveys to compare plant species composition inside and outside the deer exclosures.

Comparison of species composition along a transect from a field to a forest or from a disturbed to an undisturbed site

Species composition may change dramatically as you move from an open site, such as a field, to a closed site, such as a forest. Similarly, species may change as you move from a disturbed to an undisturbed site. Often the early successional and invasive species that prefer open areas will extend a short way into the forest due to higher light levels at the edge of a forest. Species originally present in disturbed sites may eventually invade less disturbed sites.

FIGURE 3
From Protocols to Interactive Research

| Early Detection Surveys (Protocol 1) | → | Detection of new problem species invading a watershed, park, or preserve. |

| Plot Sampling— Density and Percent Cover (Protocol 2) | → | Changes in species composition following control measures for invasive species (e.g., burning, applying herbicides, pulling up plants, biological control).

Comparison of species composition at sites where control measures have been taken and at sites left alone.

Comparison of species composition at sites where deer are excluded by a fence and at sites left alone. |

| Transect Surveys (Protocol 3) | → | Comparison of species composition along a transect from field to forest or from a disturbed to undisturbed site. |

| Measuring Decomposition Using a Microcosm (Protocols 4 and 5) | → | Comparison of decomposition rates in forest soil with and without earthworms.

Comparison of decomposition rates in litter and mineral soil.

Comparison of decomposition rates in wetland and forest soil.

Comparison of decomposition rates under varying laboratory conditions (e.g., moisture, temperature). |

Studies Using Microcosms

Comparison of decomposition rates in soil with and without earthworms

Earthworms may have a dramatic effect on decomposition and CO_2 production in forests, as well as in garden soils and compost. Students should consider factors that might affect their results, such as whether or not they are sampling from similar layers of soil and how the weight of the worms affects their soil weight measurements (they can weigh the worms before adding them to the soil).

Comparison of decomposition rates in litter and mineral soil, in wetland and forest soils, and at varying temperatures and moisture contents

Decomposition rates will vary depending on the amount and type of organic material, temperature, and moisture content. Students might want to test these and other factors such as light levels, inoculating mineral soil with different organic materials, and soil texture (e.g., sand and clay).

INQUIRY TEACHING TIPS

Choosing a Research Question

Based on their experience using the ecology protocols, students may have ideas about interesting research questions they could address using these techniques. Some teachers give students wide leeway in choosing a topic and developing appropriate research questions and strategies. Other teachers prefer to specify an overall topic, such as the population levels of invasive species in a neighborhood woodlot or park, and then encourage each student group to develop their own related research questions.

To get students started, the class should investigate what is known about invasive species in their area. There are many excellent websites to help students learn about invasive species. Students also may be able to access fact sheets on individual invasive species put out by state environmental or natural resources agencies or nonprofit environmental groups such as The Nature Conservancy. Connecting with scientists at a local university, state agency, or environmental nonprofit may also prove useful.

SCiLINKS.
THE WORLD'S A CLICK AWAY

Topic: invasive species
Go to: www.sciLINKS.org
Code: IE01

Once you have conducted an invasive species project with students, be sure to archive their reports or put the results on a website so that they will be available to students in future classes. By reviewing completed projects, students will get ideas about interesting questions as well as effective research and presentation techniques. Furthermore, if you save student research reports from one year to the next, students can design their research projects based on results and recommendations made by previous student researchers and then make their own recommendations to next year's students. Rather than each class starting their research from square one, students model professional scientific practice by starting with a review of what has already been accomplished in the field. In carrying out these steps, students not only improve their understanding of their own research, they also gain a broader understanding of the ways scientists work both individually and collaboratively.

The process of choosing a question and designing related investigations will be a new experience for students who are accustomed to traditional high school labs. Your students initially may seem frustrated with this assignment. After a period of floundering and hoping that you will help them find the "right" answer, most students will gain confidence and get accustomed to the idea of being responsible for open-ended inquiry.

Allowing Time for Exploratory Research

Contrary to popular belief, scientists do not routinely launch into research by stating and then testing a hypothesis using a controlled experiment. In many cases, they start with a period of exploration, observation, and discovery that gradually leads to ideas about fruitful areas of investigation. This is especially true in ecology, where it is important to become familiar with the ecosystem one is studying and where much research involves monitoring rather than experiments. In addition, because experiments are so difficult to conduct in the field, the number of replicates may be limited and controls may be imperfect.

If you can fit exploratory research into your class schedule, it will provide a chance for students to apply curiosity, imagination, and creativity to science rather than having to follow a predetermined set of rules. This period of trial and error also will help students discover for themselves some of the basic principles of research design, such as the need to be consistent in methods.

Based on considerations of curriculum, scheduling, and student ability levels, interactive research may consist of a single project or series of investigations. Ideally, students carry out preliminary investigations, and then use the results of these explorations to focus their question and refine their research design. They might decide to carry out additional exploratory level investigations or to use what they have learned to design a controlled experiment with a clearly defined hypothesis, dependent and independent variables, and replicates for each treatment.[*]

Research Design

Much of the research students will be conducting involves each group surveying a slightly different area. Monitoring surveys are not experiments and thus do not include samples or replicates per se. However, it is important to survey a number of sites, and students can combine data collected at different sites.

Students can conduct field experiments using the plot and transect surveys. They should be very careful to compare sites as similar as possible except for the one factor they are testing (e.g., site where invasive species has been mowed vs. site left alone, soil at sites with and without worms). Students can also conduct lab experiments using the decomposition protocols.

[*]For a thorough discussion of student research, including dependent and independent variables, treatments, and replicates, see Cothron, J. H., R. N. Giese, and R. J. Rezba. 1999. *Students and Research: Practical Strategies for Science Classrooms and Competitions*, 3rd ed. Dubuque, Iowa: Kendall/Hunt.

Questions about Protocols—Creating "Teachable Moments"

Even though we have included step-by-step instructions for the protocols, questions about exactly what to do will invariably arise while students are carrying them out. If you haven't previously guided students in research, you may be caught off guard by these questions and not know how to answer.

If this happens to you, don't panic! Making decisions about how to carry out research procedures is something scientists face all the time. Although they often consult more experienced scientists or the scientific literature, sometimes the information available is incomplete and they have to come up with their own solutions. As long as the solutions are well thought out and the relevant details are reported in the methods section of the research report, this is acceptable. Thus you can use questions you don't know the answers to—or for which there might not even be accepted answers—to engage students in finding or coming up with suitable answers on their own. This is a "teachable moment" where you can help students model how professional scientists answer such questions.

If students pose questions about methods while they are conducting research, we suggest two approaches to answering them. First, refer the students back to the protocol instructions. If nothing there helps them answer their questions, then guide them in developing answers. For example, in measuring percent cover of plants, students have asked whether they should measure cover as seen from above the plot or at ground level. One way to answer this question is to refer students back to their original research question. Are they interested in the area of the soil that is bare and thus readily available to new seeds? If so, the percent cover at soil level is important. Or are they interested in how much light is available to smaller understory plants? If this is the important question, then estimating the percent cover of leaves, stems, and trunks that may cast shade on understory plants is important.

If several students or student groups will be compiling their data together, it is important that everyone in the group follows whatever decisions are made about procedures. Standardized procedures are also important when students are comparing different sites or treatments, or data collected in different years.

In some cases, your students might be collecting data that will be shared with a scientist. For example, the *Phragmites* project described in this manual was originally set up as a collaborative project where students shared data with Cornell researchers. If you engage in such a collaborative project, you want to be sure you follow the same procedures as the scientist. If the materials the scientist has provided do not provide clear instructions, then contacting the scientist is the best way to proceed.

No matter how you guide students in answering questions on procedures, make sure they record exactly what they end up doing. This way, when new students are continuing the research in subsequent years, they can refer to procedures used by previous students, and year-to-year comparisons will be much more valid.

Results—A Look at Variability

Students may be familiar with calculating averages or means but they may not have given much thought to variability. Even if the mean is the same for two groups of plots, the variability might be different. Figures 4 and 5 both show the results of a purple loosestrife survey with an average of 10 purple loosestrife plants per m^2. Each point represents the number of purple loosestrife plants in a m^2 plot. Which site had higher variability among the different plots?

FIGURE 4
Site A

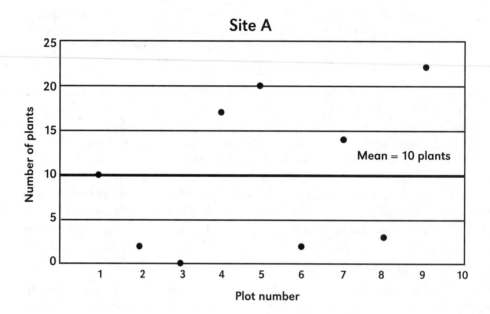

FIGURE 5
Site B

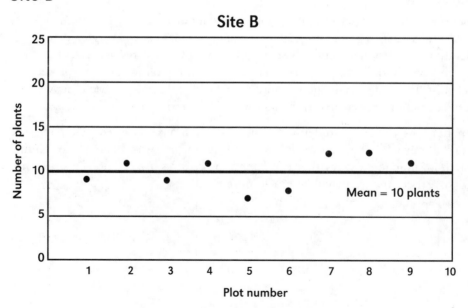

Understanding the sources of variability is essential for researchers. Variability might come from differences between the way each student or group took their measurements and from actual differences among plots.

Students may notice differences in the way they took data while they were in the field. For example, if a plant was halfway in the plot and halfway out of the plot, how did they count it? Did the other groups count such plants the same way? Are there any questions about procedures that came up while they were in the field? Did they make decisions about procedures when questions came up in their group, or did the whole class get together and decide on a procedure?

Some protocols require making more judgment calls than others and this also can contribute to variability in the results. For example, when recording percent cover, scientists make a visual estimate rather than directly count or measure plants. You can imagine that different students in your class might make these estimates slightly differently, even for the same plot. You may have noticed this in the exercise to introduce percent cover or when students were taking data in the field. One way to reduce this sort of variability is for one researcher to make the percent cover estimate for each plot. But that may be impractical given the number of plots you need to cover. Thus, practicing the protocol and making careful estimates in the field is likely the best way to reduce this type of variability.

So far, we've discussed variability according to how people collect data. This type of variability is called *experimenter error* and attempts should be made to reduce it as described above. Another source of variability in fieldwork comes from nature itself. If students surveyed ten plots, most likely the species were not present in identical numbers in each plot. For example, there might be 10 purple loosestrife plants in one plot and 50 in another, or mosses might cover 10% of the ground in one plot and 35% in another. This type of natural variability is an important part of your results. It would be wrong to try to reduce this variability by choosing plots that look alike. In fact, examining such variability may lead to a better understanding of what is occurring in nature.

Sometimes by looking at variability in their results, students might come up with questions that they could answer by thinking about what they observed in the field. Was the soil in some plots wetter than the soil in other plots? Were some plots shaded and others in the open sun? Could soil moisture, sunlight, or any other environmental factor help explain the variability in the number of plants? Students may have taken notes or data in the field (e.g., on shade) that would support their explanations or lead them to believe that their explanations are not true. For example, did the plots that they marked down as being shady have fewer garlic mustard plants than the sunny plots?

Often the questions that come up when scientists examine variability can lead to a new study. For example, if students noticed high variability in the number of purple loosestrife plants, they might hypothesize that sites that were further from the creek had fewer purple loosestrife stems than those that were close to the creek. They might be able to test their hypothesis by measuring the distance to the creek of each plot. They could then make a graph showing distance from the creek on the x-axis and number of purple loosestrife plants on the y-axis, and see if there was any relationship.

Unexpected Results

> If the result confirms the hypothesis, then you've made a measurement. If the result is contrary to the hypothesis, then you've made a discovery.
>
> —Enrico Fermi, physicist

Students are likely familiar with classroom labs that are used to demonstrate a particular principle or concept and where there is one right answer if they have followed the instructions carefully. When conducting more open-ended inquiry, students may encounter unexpected results. Because they are used to a single correct answer, students may feel they have done something wrong or even try to change their results when they encounter something unexpected. However, professional scientists often encounter unexpected results and as indicated in the above quote from Enrico Fermi, some of the most interesting discoveries are made when scientists examine critically the unexpected. Thus, it is important to engage students in a discussion of unexpected results and help them develop an explanation for these findings as well as for results that are less surprising. Unexpected results also are often used to suggest a future research direction.

Engaging in Peer Review

> Public discussions of the explanations proposed by students is a form of peer review of investigations, and peer review is an important aspect of science. Talking with peers about science experiences helps students develop meaning and understanding. Their conversations clarify the concepts and processes of science, helping students make sense of the content of science.
>
> (NRC 1996, 174)

In schools, peer review of student research reports can provide opportunities for students to think critically as they question their own and each other's research designs, assumptions, results, interpretations, and conclusions. After students have planned a research project, they will benefit from meeting in pairs or small groups to discuss their ideas and exchange written feedback. After students have completed their research projects, peer review provides a forum for critical evaluation of research results and helps students improve the quality of their reports or poster presentations.

After exchanging peer reviews, students should be encouraged to consider using the feedback to revise their research reports. To assess their understanding of the peer review process, you might ask them to address the following questions in their final write-ups:

▶ What peer review comments did you receive?

▶ Did you agree with these comments? Why or why not?

▶ How did you use the comments in preparing your final report?

To avoid unhelpful and even harmful criticisms, we have provided a number of worksheets for use in the peer review aspects of protocols and interactive research. (See pp. 174–176.) You may want to lead your students in a discussion of why peer review is important and how best to provide feedback that is helpful to their peers.[*]

Inevitably, some of your students will receive peer reviews that are not helpful, possibly even tactless or otherwise inappropriate. You might mention in a classroom discussion that this problem also occurs in professional scientific review, but that the goal for all peer reviewers should be to provide constructive criticism in order to promote better science.

---

[*]For an activity to help students understand why peer review is important, see Gift, N. and M. E. Krasny. 2003. The great fossil fiasco: Teaching students about peer review. *The American Biology Teacher* 65(3).

ASSESSMENT

PERFORMANCE ASSESSMENT

Sample questions are included after each of the first four chapters of the Student Edition, and test questions for the whole book are included on pages 42–44 of this Teacher's Guide. We also provide a series of tools for assessing performance as students design and conduct research, interpret and present results, and engage in peer review.

In assessing student research, clearly defined "right" or "wrong" answers rarely exist. Instead, the goal of assessment is to evaluate the process used by the students and the conceptual understandings they have achieved through their research experiences. Laboratory journals, worksheets, draft reports, and responses to peer review all provide evidence of the progress students have made in thinking critically, synthesizing information, and carrying out scientific research. The following pages outline possible assessment criteria for student research, as well as example assessment rubrics for research posters and reports. These can be downloaded in electronic form from the EI website so you can make adaptations to meet the needs of your particular students and their projects.

The peer review process provides both opportunities and challenges for assessment. Through peer review, some of the assessment responsibility can be shifted from the teacher to the students themselves—an important step in promoting self-initiated learning. Once students become familiar with peer review, they anticipate the expectations of other students carrying out projects similar to their own. This may motivate them to work harder and to look more critically at their work.

Because keeping track of all the comments exchanged by students may be too cumbersome, we suggest you focus on determining how students respond to the feedback they receive. This approach helps overcome any worries among students about whether it is fair to be evaluated by someone other than their teacher. If they don't agree with reviewers' suggestions, that's fine, as long as they can justify their positions. In their final research reports, you can direct students to summarize the comments they received from peer reviewers, state whether they agreed with these critiques, and explain how they would use them in revising their work.

SCI LINKS.
THE WORLD'S A CLICK AWAY

Topic: assessment
Go to: *www.scilinks.org*
Code: IE08

EXAMPLE ASSESSMENT RUBRICS FOR EI STUDENT RESEARCH

Assessment Criteria for Student Research

Criteria such as these can be the basis of a checklist for students and a grading rubric for completed research portfolios.

Identify a Researchable Question
- ❏ Develop a clearly stated, researchable question.
- ❏ Include a clear statement of why this question is relevant to ecology or invasive species issues.
- ❏ Review previous work in the field, including Internet as well as text-based sources.
- ❏ Where appropriate, include clearly stated hypotheses.

Plan the Investigation for All Research
- ❏ Clearly show how methods address the research question(s).
- ❏ Describe appropriate methods to gather, interpret, and analyze the data within constraints of time and resources.
- ❏ Identify safety concerns and precautions that will be taken.

If Conducting Experimental Research
- ❏ Identify treatments and a control.
- ❏ Vary only one independent variable at a time.
- ❏ Use adequate replicates of each treatment.

Conduct the Research
- ❏ Carefully follow the protocols and other procedures.
- ❏ Use proper equipment and safety precautions.
- ❏ Make reasoned decisions when questions come up about procedures.
- ❏ Carefully record data and relevant observations.
- ❏ Document any decisions made about research design or data collection as the research progresses.

Analyze the Data
- ❏ Clearly summarize data using tables and graphs.
- ❏ Identify trends and data that do not fit the trends.
- ❏ Identify potential sources of variability.

Interpret the Results and Formulate Conclusions
- ❏ Clearly state the meaning of the results in terms of the original research question.
- ❏ Identify possible improvements in the research design.
- ❏ Identify questions the research is not able to address.
- ❏ Suggest new directions for future research.
- ❏ Compare results to results achieved by others who have conducted similar research.
- ❏ Compare actual results to predicted results where appropriate.

Present the Project and Engage in Peer Review
- ❏ Effectively communicate the research design and results to a peer audience.
- ❏ Defend or revise conclusions based on considering alternative explanations of research results.
- ❏ Revise written report or poster presentation based on reviewers' comments.

Assessment Rubrics for Poster Presentations

Name(s) of student(s) _____

Date _____

ASSESSMENT SCALE
1—Inadequate in meeting requirements of the task
2—Minimal in meeting requirements of the task
3—Adequate in meeting requirements of the task
4—Superior in meeting requirements of the task

Poster Presentation Criteria	Evaluation	Points
Poster includes these sections: Title, Research Question, Hypothesis (if appropriate), Procedure, Results, Conclusions, and Acknowledgments (if appropriate).	1 2 3 4	
Purpose is clearly stated in the research question.	1 2 3 4	
Procedure is described clearly enough to be reproduced.	1 2 3 4	
Results and conclusions are displayed in a manner that is easy to follow.	1 2 3 4	
Display is neat, clearly labeled, and easy to read.	1 2 3 4	
Ideas fit together and make sense.	1 2 3 4	
	TOTAL	

ASSESSMENT SCALE
Assign "?" if there is not enough information to decide.
Assign 5 points for each "Yes" and 0 points for each "No" or "?"

Research Design Criteria	Evaluation	Points
Research was appropriately designed for answering the question.	Yes No ?	
Methods were clearly suitable for answering the question.	Yes No ?	
Results focus on the original research question.	Yes No ?	
Conclusions appear well supported by the data.	Yes No ?	
If the research was an experiment, answer the questions below.		
Only one independent variable was changed at a time.	Yes No ?	
There was a control treatment or reference site, which was exposed to the same conditions as the treatments except for the independent variable (as nearly as possible).	Yes No ?	
Adequate replicates were provided for each treatment.	Yes No ?	
	TOTAL	

Assessment Rubrics for Written Reports

Name(s) of student(s) _____

Date _____

<table>
<tr><td colspan="3" align="center">ASSESSMENT SCALE
1—Inadequate in meeting requirements of the task
2—Minimal in meeting requirements of the task
3—Adequate in meeting requirements of the task
4—Superior in meeting requirements of the task</td></tr>
</table>

Criteria	Evaluation	Points
Introduction	1 2 3 4	
States a researchable question.	1 2 3 4	
Clearly explains why this question is relevant to ecology and invasive species.	1 2 3 4	
Summarizes previous work related to the research question, if applicable.	1 2 3 4	
States a hypothesis that addresses the research question and expected results (if appropriate).	1 2 3 4	
Procedure		
Experiment is appropriately designed to address the research question.	1 2 3 4	
Describes procedures clearly enough to be replicated.	1 2 3 4	
Uses proper equipment, methods, and safety precautions.	1 2 3 4	
Includes taking data and making relevant observations.	1 2 3 4	
If the research was an experiment, answer the questions below.		
Includes independent and dependent variables and a control or reference site, which was exposed to the same conditions as the treatments except for the independent variable (as nearly as possible).	1 2 3 4	
Changes only one independent variable between treatments.	1 2 3 4	
Provides adequate replicates of each treatment.	1 2 3 4	
Results		
Summarizes data clearly using tables and graphs.	1 2 3 4	
Describes important trends.	1 2 3 4	
Discusses potential sources of variability.	1 2 3 4	

Conclusions		
Compares actual results to predicted results, if appropriate.	1 2 3 4	
Clearly discusses meaning of the results in terms of the original research question.	1 2 3 4	
Makes conclusions that are well supported by the data.	1 2 3 4	
Identifies possible improvements in the research design.	1 2 3 4	
Suggests new directions for future research.	1 2 3 4	
Defends or revises conclusions based on consideration of alternative explanations of research results.	1 2 3 4	
Overall Report		
Displays understanding of research design.	1 2 3 4	
Displays understanding of applicable concepts in ecology.	1 2 3 4	
Includes clear discussion of use of peer review comments in revising the report, or logical argument for why peer suggestions were not followed.	1 2 3 4	
Appropriately cites written and/or web-based references.	1 2 3 4	
Is neat, organized, and well written.	1 2 3 4	
Organizes ideas clearly.	1 2 3 4	
Uses proper spelling and grammar.	1 2 3 4	
	TOTAL	

SAMPLE TEST QUESTIONS

1. Which of the following statements are true?

   (a) Some species native to North America become invasive. (T)

   (b) All invasive species are species that are introduced from other continents. (F)

   (c) Most invasive species in North America have been introduced from other continents. (T)

   (d) Most species that are introduced to North America from other continents become invasive. (F)

2. Emilia is a park manager and discovers a small patch of the invasive species garlic mustard along the edge of the woods. What should Emilia do if she wants to protect the native species in her park from this invasive plant? Why should she do this?

   Emilia should try to get rid of the garlic mustard immediately, because seeds of species in small patches can easily land outside the patch and germinate in areas not yet invaded by the invasive species.

3. What are some of the negative impacts of invasive species?

   ▶ *Invasive species are a major cause of loss of biodiversity.*

   ▶ *When an invasive species wipes out native species, people whose livelihoods depend on the native species can be affected.*

   ▶ *Invasive species prey on native species.*

   ▶ *Invasive species outcompete native species.*

   ▶ *Invasive species may change ecosystems to make them unfavorable for native and other desirable species.*

4. Describe some of the characteristics of plant species that allow them to become invasive. What characteristics would you expect an invasive animal species to have?

   Plants—

   ▶ *They grow rapidly and compete with other plants.*

   ▶ *They produce large numbers of seeds at a young age.*

   ▶ *Their seeds can survive a long time before sprouting.*

   ▶ *Their seeds travel long distances.*

   ▶ *They can spread by sprouting from the roots or stems.*

   ▶ *They have few predators.*

   ▶ *Their native region has a climate similar to that of the U.S.*

Animals—

▶ *They have few or no predators.*

▶ *They have an ample food supply.*

▶ *They have high reproduction rates.*

5. List questions related to invasive species that each of the following types of ecologists might be interested in: population ecologists, community ecologists, and ecosystem ecologists.

▶ *Population ecologists study the changes in numbers and location of organisms. A population ecologist studying purple loosestrife might ask questions such as: How many purple loosestrife plants are there in a particular region? Is the number of purple loosestrife plants increasing or decreasing? Why? Where are purple loosestrife plants found?*

▶ *Community ecologists ask questions about the interaction of different organisms. What effect do biological control insects have on the populations of an invasive species? Does purple loosestrife compete with cattails? Do birds prey on the insects colonizing Phragmites? After herbicides reduce the population of an invasive species, what plants will invade or reinvade the site? How do the species of plants change as one moves from a disturbed to a more natural site?*

▶ *Ecosystem ecologists ask questions about the interactions of living things with their nonliving environment. What is the effect of introduced earthworms on organic matter decomposition in forest soils? What is the effect of tamarisk on the hydrology of desert streams? What is the effect of zebra mussels on water clarity in lakes?*

6. Draw a population growth curve for an invasive species first colonizing a new area. Draw a population growth curve for an invasive species over 20 years. What factors might influence the population growth of an invasive species in the short and long term?

An invasive species first entering an area will often show exponential growth. Eventually limiting factors (such as lack of space, food, or water, competition, or introduction of predators) will slow the population growth, resulting in a logistic growth curve.

7. A major forest fire has just destroyed a forest. Diagram how you think this site will change over the next hundred years.

The site will likely first be invaded by grasses and other herbaceous species (often these are introduced species). Next we can expect shrubby species to dominate. Over the long term, trees colonizing the site will become large enough to dominate.

8. How might an invasive species change nutrient and carbon cycles? How might they change food webs?

   Zebra mussels filter nutrients out of the water, thus making them unavailable to other organisms. The lack of nutrients can cause declines in phytoplankton (primary producer) populations and have effects on the entire food web. Earthworms rapidly break down organic material in soils, which may cause some of the nitrogen to be leached into groundwater or surface water and become unavailable to other soil organisms and plants. Introduced species, such as the opossum shrimp, can prey on species lower in the food web, thus destroying a source of food for other animals in the food web.

9. Claire and Rafael plan to raise and release beetles that are used in the biological control of purple loosestrife. They also want to follow the impact of the beetles on the purple loosestrife in a wetland near their school. Outline a plan for monitoring the impact of the beetles on purple loosestrife.

   (a) Conduct a survey of the release site using plot sampling prior to releasing the beetles. If possible, set up permanent plots at the site.

   (b) Repeat the survey over a number of years after releasing the beetles to document any changes in vegetation.

   (c) Also compare sites where beetles were released and not released to see if any changes in plant species are likely due to the beetles or to weather, or to other successional changes.

10. Mrs. Potter's science class has been asked by a local nature preserve to survey the preserve for the presence of garlic mustard, which the preserve manager thinks may be present in the preserve. What factors would you consider in designing the survey?

    (a) At what time of year is garlic mustard most noticeable? (Surveys in winter or fall might miss the garlic mustard because it won't be obvious.)

    (b) Are there any disturbed sites (e.g., roadsides, trails) where garlic mustard might initially invade?

    (c) Are there any travel corridors (e.g., railroad tracks, trails, roads) where garlic mustard might initially invade?

    (d) How might the preserve manager measure the size of the patches of garlic mustard? (If the patches are still small, it might be possible to pull the plants up by the roots before they become widespread.)

    (e) Does the preserve manager need detailed information or does she just need to know the locations of patches? If she doesn't need detailed information, Mrs. Potter's class can recommend an early detection survey but if she needs lots of information, the class might recommend plot sampling or a transect survey.

REFERENCES

ASIAN LONGHORNED BEETLE

Haack, R., K. Law, V. Mastro, H. Ossenbruggen, and B. Raimo. 1997. New York's battle with the Asian longhorned beetle. *Journal of Forestry* 95: 11–15.

Milius, S. 1999. Son of long-horned beetles. *Science News* 155: 380–382.

BIOLOGICAL CONTROL

Blossey, B. 2000. A plan for developing biological control of *Phragmites australis* in North America. *Wetland Issues* 12: 23–28.

Blossey, B. et al. 2001. Nontarget feeding of leaf-beetles introduced to control purple loosestrife (*Lythrum salicaria L.*). *Natural Areas Journal* 21: 368–377.

Blossey, B. et al. 2001. Developing biological control of *Alliaria petiolata* [M. Bieb.] Cavara and Grande (Garlic Mustard). *Natural Areas Journal* 21: 357–367.

Blossey, B. and L. Skinner. 2001. Design and importance of post-release monitoring. *Proceedings of the X International Symposium on Biological Control of Weeds.* Bozeman, Mont.: Montana State University.

Hokkanen, M. and J. Lynch (eds.). 1995. *Biological control: Risks and benefits.* Cambridge, England: Cambridge University Free Press.

Malecki, R. et al. 1993. Biological control of purple loosestrife. *BioScience* 43: 680–686.

CHESTNUT BLIGHT

Davis, D. *Where There Are Mountains: An Environmental History of the Southern Appalachians.* Athens, Ga.: The University of Georgia Press.

DEER

Waller, D. and W. Alverson. 1997. The white-tailed deer: A keystone herbivore. *Wildlife Society Bulletin* 25: 217–226.

EARTHWORMS

Alban, D. and E. Berry. 1994. Effect of earthworm invasion on morphology, carbon, and nitrogen of a forest soil. *Applied Soil Ecology* 1: 243–249.

Gurwick, N. and M. Krasny. 2001. Enhancing student understanding of environmental sciences research. *The American Biology Teacher* 63: 236–241.

Nixon, W. 1995. As the worm turns. *American Forests* (autumn) 34–36.

Steinberg, D., R. Pouyat, R. Parmelee, and P. Groffman. 1997. Earthworm abundance and nitrogen mineralization rates along an urban-rural land use gradient. *Soil Biology and Biochemistry* 29: 427–430.

ECOLOGY

Ricklefs, R. 1990. *Ecology*. New York: W. H. Freeman.

INQUIRY-BASED SCIENCE

National Research Council. 1996. *National Science Education Standards*. Washington, D.C.: National Academy Press.

National Research Council. 2000. *Inquiry and the National Science Education Standards*. Washington, D.C.: National Academy Press.

INVASIVE SPECIES

Federal Interagency Committee for the Management of Noxious and Exotic Weeds. 1998. *Invasive Plants: Changing the Landscape of America*. Washington, D.C.

Karieva, P. (ed.) 1996. Developing a predictive ecology for nonindigenous species and ecological invasions. Special feature in *Ecology* 77(6): 1651–1679.

Luken, J. and J. Thieret (eds.). 1997. *Assessment and management of plant invasions*. Springer-Verlag.

Mack, R. et al. 2000. Biotic invasions: Causes, epidemiology, global consequences, and control. *Issues in Ecology* 5. Ecological Society of America.

National Invasive Species Council. 2001. *National Management Plan*. Washington, D.C.

Pimentel, D. et al. 2000. Environmental and economic costs of nonindigenous species in the United States. *BioScience* 50: 53–64.

Vitousek, P. 1990. Biological invasions and ecosystem processes: Towards an integration of population biology and ecosystem studies. *Oikos* 57: 7–13.

MICROCOSMS

Taylor, B. and D. Parkinson. 1988. A new microcosm approach to litter decomposition studies. *Canadian Journal of Botany* 66: 1933–1939.

Tilman, D. 1977. Resource competition between planktonic algae—experimental and theoretical approach. *Ecology* 58 (2): 338–348.

PHRAGMITES

(See also **Biological Control.**)

Marks, M., B. Lapin, and J. Randall. *Element Stewardship Abstract for* Phragmites australis. Arlington: The Nature Conservancy.

PURPLE LOOSESTRIFE

(See also **Biological Control.**)

Blossey, B., L. Skinner, and J. Taylor. 2001. Impact and management of purple loosestrife (*Lythrum salicaria*) in North America. *Biodiversity and Conservation* 10: 1787–1807.

TAMARISK

Carpenter, A. *Element Stewardship Abstract for Tamarisk*. 1998. Arlington: The Nature Conservancy.

ZEBRA MUSSEL

Mills, E. et al. 1994. Exotic species and the integrity of the Great Lakes. *BioScience* 44: 666–676.

O'Neill, Jr., C. and A. Dextrase. 1993. *The Zebra Mussel—Its Origin and Spread in North America*. Brockport, N.Y.: New York Sea Grant Institute, State University of New York-Brockport.

O'Neill, C. 2001. *The National Aquatic Nuisance Species Clearinghouse and Searchable Electronic Database*. Brockport, N.Y.: New York Sea Grant, State University of New York-Brockport.

CORNELL SCIENTIFIC INQUIRY SERIES
STUDENT EDITION

Invasion
Ecology

NSTApress®
NATIONAL SCIENCE TEACHERS ASSOCIATION

CORNELL SCIENTIFIC INQUIRY SERIES

STUDENT EDITION

Invasion Ecology

BY THE ENVIRONMENTAL INQUIRY LEADERSHIP TEAM
MARIANNE KRASNY
NANCY TRAUTMANN
WILLIAM CARLSEN
CHRISTINE CUNNINGHAM

WITH CORNELL SCIENTIST DR. BERND BLOSSEY
ALAN FIERO (FARNSWORTH MIDDLE SCHOOL)
ADAM WELMAN

NATIONAL SCIENCE TEACHERS ASSOCIATION

NATIONAL SCIENCE TEACHERS ASSOCIATION

Claire Reinburg, Director
Judy Cusick, Associate Editor
Carol Duval, Associate Editor
Betty Smith, Associate Editor

ART AND DESIGN Linda Olliver, Director
    Cover image by Bernd Blossey, Cornell University
PRINTING AND PRODUCTION Catherine Lorrain-Hale, Director
    Nguyet Tran, Assistant Production Manager
    Jack Parker, Desktop Publishing Specialist
PUBLICATIONS OPERATIONS Erin Miller, Manager
MARKETING Holly Hemphill, Director
NSTA WEB Tim Weber, Webmaster
PERIODICALS PUBLISHING Shelley Carey, Director
sciLINKS Tyson Brown, Manager
NATIONAL SCIENCE TEACHERS ASSOCIATION
Gerald F. Wheeler, Executive Director
David Beacom, Publisher

Invasion Ecology
    NSTA Stock Number: PB162X4S
    ISBN: 0-87355-211-3
    Library of Congress Catalog Card Number: 98-84914
    Printed in the USA by Victor Graphics
    Printed on recycled paper

Library of Congress of Cataloging-in-Publication Data
Invasion ecology / Marianne Krasny and the Environmental Inquiry Team— Student edition.
    p. cm. — (Cornell scientific inquiry series)
    ISBN 0-87355-211-3
    1. Biology invasions. I. Krasny, Marianne E. II. Series.
    QH353.I5835 2002
    577'.18—dc21   2002011620

This material is based on the work supported by the National Science Foundation under Grant No. 96-18142. Any opinions, findings, conclusions or recommendations expressed in this material are those of the authors and do not necessarily reflect the views of the National Science Foundation.

Table of Contents
STUDENT EDITION

SECTION 1. UNDERSTANDING INVASION ECOLOGY

Section 2. Invasion Ecology Protocols— Introducing Research

Section 3. Beyond Protocols— Conducting Interactive Research

How can you and your students avoid searching hundreds of science web sites to locate the best sources of information on a given topic? SciLinks, created and maintained by the National Science Teachers Association (NSTA), has the answer.

In a SciLinked text, such as this one, you'll find a logo and keyword near a concept your class is studying, a URL (*www.scilinks.org*), and a keyword code. Simply go to the SciLinks website, type in the code, and receive an annotated listing of as many as 15 web pages—all of which have gone through an extensive review process conducted by a team of science educators. SciLinks is your best source of pertinent, trustworthy Internet links on subjects from astronomy to zoology.

Need more information? Take a tour—*http://www.scilinks.org/tour/*

PREFACE

WHY STUDY ECOLOGY OF INVASIVE SPECIES?

Just yesterday, I heard a report on the radio that the U.S. was cutting off all imports of clementines from Spain. I love clementines—those small oranges that come in a wooden box and are easy to peel. But at the same time I can understand the seriousness of the problem that led to the ban on imports. The Mediterranean fruit fly, a European insect that has destroyed U.S. citrus orchards in the past, had just been found on clementines coming into the U.S. from Spain. Could this small fly once again spread to orchards in California and elsewhere, destroying our citrus crop?

The Mediterranean fruit fly is only one of many pest species that have been introduced to North America from other continents. In addition to insects, introduced problem species include plants and mammals, such as rats, which eat crops and stored food. Even tiny microbes can cause major damage to forests, crops, and human health. Some examples include the chestnut blight fungus, which wiped out chestnut trees in eastern forests, and the West Nile virus, which has killed humans and birds.

How does a newly introduced species become a problem in a natural ecosystem, such as a forest, wetland, or lake? How can we predict which species might harm native plants, animals, and entire ecosystems? What kind of harm do these species cause? What can we do to control species that do become problems?

Ecology is a science that helps us understand how living things interact with each other and with the nonliving parts of the environment. Learning about ecology can help us understand how some introduced species spread and how they impact the environment. It also can help us control invasive species. By controlling problem species, we can reduce their impact on forests, wetlands, and other areas that we would like to protect.

CARRYING OUT YOUR OWN RESEARCH

This book is part of the Environmental Inquiry series developed at Cornell University. The Environmental Inquiry books provide opportunities for you to learn about ecology and other environmental subjects. In addition, they provide opportunities for you to conduct scientific research on real-life environmental issues. Using the research techniques in this book, you will learn to investigate what invasive species are in your area and how they might be impacting local ecosystems. Professional scientists use these same research techniques to answer questions about invasive species and other ecological topics.

Through your Environmental Inquiry research experiences, you will learn to ask your own questions and to investigate the answers. You also will gain an understanding of how professional scientists go about solving environmental problems. Many people believe that scientists are able to conduct experiments to find the answers to any new environmental questions that pop up. The public and politicians may get frustrated and even make fun of scientists who can't provide them with immediate answers to problems ranging from the impact of invasive species to global warming. In fact, it is nearly impossible to conduct a single experiment to answer many environmental questions. (How would you design an experiment to determine whether or not the Mediterranean fruit fly will spread to and destroy orchards in the U.S?) Instead, ecologists usually conduct several different kinds of research and piece together the results to come up with the best possible answer.

As you conduct your own research, you may find yourself coming up with only part of the answer to your original question. Likely you will have new questions that can only be answered by additional research. Don't worry—that's the way science works! Science is a continuous process of discovery, and there is always more to be learned. This is what makes science creative and exciting!

Many people also don't realize that, rather than working alone, most scientists are constantly communicating with their peers. In fact, these communications are an essential part of conducting good science. Scientists discuss ideas with their peers, give each other feedback on research plans and reports, and work together on joint research projects. As you go about conducting research on invasive species, you and your classroom "peer scientists" will help each other come up with good research questions, choose appropriate techniques to answer these questions, and think about how to analyze and interpret your findings.

INVASION ECOLOGY STUDENT EDITION

This book is designed with two purposes in mind. First, we hope you will learn some of the basic principles of ecology and how they can be applied to studying and managing invasive species. Second, this book will help you experience some of the ways in which scientists work together to conduct research.

Section 1 introduces you to the science of ecology and invasive species. With the understanding you gain from these four chapters, you may find yourself asking questions about invasive species in your area. Section 2 includes seven research protocols—these are instructions for techniques you can use to answer questions about ecology and invasive species. Section 3 includes instructions for two research projects that students have carried out in cooperation with Cornell scientists and that you also may be interested in trying. This section also suggests ideas for research projects you could conduct using the ecology protocols you have learned. At the back of the book is a collection of worksheets designed to guide your progress through the various steps of designing and conducting research, including exchanging feedback with fellow students.

As you make your way through your ecology research, we encourage you to visit our website *http://ei.cornell.edu* to share your experiences, observations, and questions with other participating students. Have fun, and good luck with your research!

—Marianne Krasny
Lead Author

UNDERSTANDING INVASION ECOLOGY

CHAPTER 1

INTRODUCTION

**Declaration of Emergency—
Asian Longhorned Beetle**

Federal Register: March 15, 1999

DEPARTMENT OF AGRICULTURE

Office of the Secretary

Declaration of Emergency because of the Asian longhorned beetle

A serious outbreak of the Asian longhorned beetle, *Anoplophora glabripennis*, is occurring in Illinois and New York.

The Asian longhorned beetle, an insect native to China, Japan, Korea, and the Isle of Hainan, is a destructive pest of hardwood trees. It is known to attack healthy maple, horse chestnut, birch, rose of Sharon, poplar, willow, elm, locust, mulberry, chinaberry, apple, cherry, pear, and citrus trees. It may also attack other species of hardwood trees. ...If this pest moves into the hardwood forests of the United States, the nursery and forest products industry could experience severe economic losses.

In cooperation with the States of Illinois and New York, the Animal and Plant Health Inspection Service (APHIS) has initiated a program to eradicate the Asian longhorned beetle. ... However, APHIS resources are insufficient to meet the estimated $5.5 million needed for the Federal share. ...

Therefore, ... I declare that there is an emergency, which threatens the forest and maple syrup industries of this country.

Dan Glickman

Secretary of Agriculture

Can you imagine our cities with no maple trees lining the streets? Our hardwood forests with no poplar or birch trees? Our wetlands without willows? Our fruit tree orchards destroyed? This is the threat U.S. Secretary of Agriculture Dan Glickman felt was posed by a single species of insect—the Asian longhorned beetle. And many scientists agree with him.

How can a single species of insect pose such a threat to millions of acres of forests, orchards, and street trees? What can we do about the Asian longhorned beetle and other plants and animals that invade our farms, cities, and forests? The study of ecology helps us to find answers to these questions. Through applying ecological principles and conducting research, scientists are learning to manage *invasive species* such as the Asian longhorned beetle. Students can learn alongside the scientists and, in some cases, help them.

WHAT ARE INVASIVE SPECIES?

Invasive species are organisms that become widespread and threaten other organisms and ecosystems.

Invasive species are plants, animals, fungi, or microorganisms that spread rapidly and cause harm to other species. Sometimes invasive species threaten entire ecosystems. Although some invasive species are native to North America, most are brought in from other continents. The Asian longhorned beetle, for example, was introduced to the U.S. in wooden packaging material that traveled on ships from Asia. Because scientists and land managers fear this beetle will spread widely and kill many trees, they are taking radical measures to control it.

WHAT IS THE SCIENCE OF ECOLOGY?

You have undoubtedly studied biology and know that biologists are concerned with living things such as plants, animals, and bacteria. Some of you also may have studied Earth science, chemistry, or physics, all of which are referred to as *physical sciences* and focus on the nonliving parts of our environment.

Ecology combines the life sciences and physical sciences. It is concerned with how organisms interact with each other and with their physical environment. Organisms interact in a number of ways. For example, they may compete for physical resources such as water, light, space, and nutrients. Animals may prey on other animals, such as when a bird eats an insect, or feed on plants, such as when beetles feed on trees. In some cases, organisms have relationships that are mutually beneficial, such as when ants drink a plant's nectar and fend off insects that might feed on the plant's flowers, stems, or leaves.

Organisms also may change the physical environment, such as when beavers build dams that create flooded wetlands or when earthworms create tunnels in the ground. Through these and other interactions, organisms affect how fast other organisms grow and reproduce.

Similarly, physical factors can determine how fast plants and animals grow and reproduce. For example, lack of water or light can slow down plant

Topic: invasive species
Go to: *www.sciLINKS.org*
Code: IE01
Topic: ecology
Go to: *www.sciLINKS.org*
Code: IE02

growth. Animals that require large territories, such as bears, may suffer when the amount of land available to them is restricted.

Ecology is important for all of us—not just those who live in the countryside. For example, understanding ecology can help us develop methods for controlling the Asian longhorned beetle and prevent it from killing trees in cities, suburbs, and rural forests.

TYPES OF ECOLOGY

Ecologists are interested in lots of different questions. Some ecologists study where plants and animals are located across the landscape. Others investigate how organisms interact with each other. Still others are interested in how nutrients cycle between living organisms and the nonliving environment. Although there are many approaches to studying ecology, the three main branches are population, community, and ecosystem ecology.

Population ecologists study the changes in numbers and location of organisms. A population ecologist studying beetles might ask questions such as: How many beetles are there in a particular region? Is the number of beetles increasing or decreasing? Why? Where are beetles found within a forest or a city park?

But beetles also interact with other animals and plants. For example, beetles live in and feed on trees. Birds and squirrels may eat the beetles, and fungi and bacteria decompose them after they die. The study of the interaction of different organisms is called *community ecology*.

Ecosystem ecologists ask questions about the interactions of living things with their nonliving environments. They may conduct research on how carbon, water, and nutrients move or cycle between the soil, organisms, and the atmosphere. For example, an ecosystem ecologist studying an area with an outbreak of beetles might wonder how trees killed by beetles will decompose and affect local carbon, water, and nitrogen cycles. Ecosystem ecologists also study how nutrients control the rate at which new plant material is produced. For example, if many trees die suddenly and decay, the nutrients that are released could cause a rapid increase in the amount of new plant material, or biomass, produced.

INTRODUCED, INVASIVE SPECIES

Ecologists hope that by learning about populations, communities, and ecosystems, they can help find solutions for environmental problems. One of the biggest environmental problems facing North America is the introduction of non-native species from other continents (also called introduced, nonindigenous, alien, or exotic species) that later become weeds or pests.

But not all alien species become problems. In fact, many introduced species bring important benefits to agriculture. For example, 98% of the U.S. food supply comes from introduced plants and animals, including wheat, rice, cattle, and poultry.

Ecology is the study of how organisms interact with each other and with their physical environment.

The three main branches of ecology are *population*, *community*, and *ecosystem ecology*.

Most invasive species have been brought into North America from other continents.

Many introduced species bring benefits to agriculture. Only a few become invasive and cause problems.

Of every 100 exotic species introduced to North America, it is estimated that only 10 are able to survive outside of cultivation. About 1 in every 10 species that survives outside of cultivation turns into a serious pest. Thus, about 1% of the species that are introduced causes serious problems (Figure 1.1). These introduced species invade gardens, agricultural fields, urban parks, and natural areas such as wetlands, forests, and grasslands. They can cause great harm to desirable plants and animals and to entire ecosystems. In fact, the environmental damage caused by such species has been estimated at $138 billion per year. Although most invasive species that cause problems are introduced from other continents, native species, such as wild grapes and black locust trees, also may become invasive.

FIGURE 1.1
Number of Exotic Species That Become Invasive

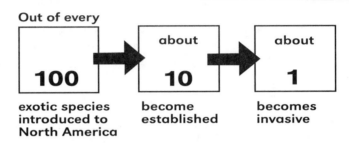

Out of every

100 exotic species introduced to North America

→ about **10** become established

→ about **1** becomes invasive

What are some introduced species that have become invasive? Some of you may have heard of kudzu in the southeastern U.S., zebra mussels in lakes and rivers of the East and Midwest, and red fire ants in the South and in Hawaii. Many of these species have significant biological, economic, social, and even health impacts. We will discuss a few examples of introduced, invasive species below.

Zebra Mussels

Zebra mussels are a freshwater shellfish, similar to clams and oysters. They were introduced to the U.S. from Russia. The mussels first entered North America in about 1986 with ballast water dumped into the Great Lakes from a foreign ship. (Ballast water is used to provide balance for ships crossing the open ocean and is often dumped upon arrival in port.) Since then, zebra mussels have been transported by boats and boat trailers to numerous lakes and rivers. Within six years after entering North American waters, zebra mussels had spread to all the Great Lakes and had entered eight large river systems.

FIGURE 1.2
Zebra Mussels

Zebra mussels reproduce rapidly and coat rocky and other hard surfaces in the water, including the shells of native mussels. This reduces the populations of native mussels. Zebra mussels also clog intake pipes for power plants and water supplies. By 1991, just five years after they were introduced, zebra mussels had caused over $3 billion worth of damage. That figure continues to rise.

Chestnut Blight

Sometimes an introduced species can have major impacts on the way of life or culture of an entire group of people. At the beginning of the twentieth century, rural communities in the eastern U.S. depended on the American chestnut tree for many of their needs. In fact, it seemed as if their entire lives revolved around the chestnut. They used the nuts for food for themselves and their hogs. The wildlife they hunted—including squirrels, wild turkeys, white-tailed deer, bear, raccoon, and grouse—also ate chestnuts. Everything from homes to furniture, coffins, musical instruments, and tools was constructed from chestnut lumber. The wood also was made into charcoal for heating, and tannin, a chemical from the bark, was used for tanning animal hides to make leather. People in the rural mountain communities were poor and the American chestnut allowed them to live where few other resources were available (Figure 1.3).

FIGURE 1.3
American Chestnut Range

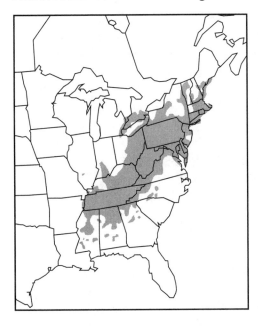

In 1904 a fungus was discovered at the Bronx Zoo in New York City. It had entered the U.S. accidentally along with Asian chestnut seedlings that people wanted to plant in this country. The Asian chestnut had evolved with the fungus for thousands of years and had developed the ability to resist the fungus. However, the American chestnut had never encountered this alien fungus and had not developed resistance. The fungus caused a disease known as the chestnut blight, which spread from New York City throughout the eastern forests, wiping out the American chestnut.

Along with the chestnut went the rural, subsistence way of life that had depended on this species. Many people left the area or had to find other ways to survive.

Asian Longhorned Beetle

At the turn of the twenty-first century, we are again seeing an introduced species that has the potential to dramatically impact forests and a rural way of life that depends on these forests. In August 1996, a man noticed large holes in the bark of the Norway maples lining his street in Brooklyn, New York. He also reported seeing large black and white beetles with long antennae coming out of these holes.

The next day, a New York City forester sent the unknown insects to Cornell University to be identified. A scientist identified them as Asian longhorned beetles. It is assumed that they arrived in the U.S. on container ships in wooden packaging material from China. A second infestation was discovered in Long Island, New York on infested trees that were sold as firewood. During summer 1998, Asian longhorned beetles were discovered in Chicago. Since then, new infestations have been found, including Central Park in New York City. All trees known to be infested have been destroyed, but it is possible that beetle larvae may be living undetected in nearby trees or other areas.

FIGURE 1.4
Asian Longhorned Beetle

Because ecologists do not understand everything about invasive species, we cannot predict whether the Asian longhorned beetle will expand its populations rapidly. However, if the Asian longhorned beetle became invasive, it could destroy hardwood trees throughout the northeastern U.S. and eastern Canada, and it seems to particularly favor maple trees. Similar to the American chestnut, maple trees are a source of food (maple syrup) and timber for rural residents. Sales of maple syrup often provide the extra income that allows farmers to keep their farms. Thus, the Asian longhorned beetle has the potential to cause major economic impact in a manner similar to the chestnut blight.

INVASIVE SPECIES THREATEN BIODIVERSITY

Biodiversity refers to the variety of organisms living in an area.

Zebra mussels, chestnut blight, and Asian longhorned beetles are all examples of invasive species that have major social and economic impacts. Invasive species also are a major cause of loss of *biodiversity*. Biodiversity refers to the variety of organisms living in an area. The higher the number of species, the higher the biodiversity. Although we often hear about loss of biodiversity in the Tropics, it is also a problem in North America.

Why does biodiversity matter? Many people value biodiversity for its own sake. These people feel there is value in having a diversity of species on Earth,

8

regardless of whether we get any direct benefit from these species. In fact, Harvard biologist E.O. Wilson has coined the term *biophilia* to describe the sense of connection to nature that many humans feel.

Topic: biodiversity
Go to: *www.sciLINKS.org*
Code: IE03

There are also practical reasons for maintaining biodiversity. Humans have always depended on the world's organisms for food, shelter, and medicine. If biodiversity decreases and species become extinct, we may lose important resources. For example, many of our important medicines come from plants. In the 1970s, scientists discovered that a small plant in Madagascar, the rosy periwinkle, contains chemicals that inhibit cancer cell growth. If this periwinkle had become extinct before 1970, researchers would not have discovered its properties, and doctors would be less effective in the fight against cancer. It is possible that endangered plants throughout the world have benefits not yet discovered by scientists.

Current extinction rates are one thousand to ten thousand times higher than before extensive human influence. This massive loss of biodiversity may threaten entire ecosystems. For example, bees are important pollinators of many agricultural and wild plants. Recent declines in the numbers of native bees might result in a loss of pollinators for plants. If a pollinator becomes extinct, the plants it pollinates also may be lost from the ecosystem. This in turn could impact the insects and other animals that rely on the lost organisms for food or shelter. Loss of the plant and animal species could impact how nutrients are cycled from plants to other organisms, and to the soil and atmosphere.

When the American chestnut disappeared from eastern forests, we lost an important component of biodiversity. Similarly, when zebra mussels take over the habitat of native species of mussels, the native shellfish disappear and biodiversity declines. Currently, about 950 species are on the U.S. Threatened and Endangered Species List. About 400 of these are at risk of extinction due to the impacts of introduced species. In fact, introduced, invasive species are the second major cause of loss of biodiversity in North America. The most important cause of declining biodiversity is loss of habitat due to development by humans (e.g., draining wetlands, paving over natural areas).

Introduced, invasive species are the second major cause of biodiversity loss in North America.

Invasive species cause a loss of biodiversity in a number of ways, including competition, predation, herbivory, and changing habitats and ecosystems. *Competition* refers to the negative impact one species or organism has on another species or organism, when they both rely on the same resources, which are in limited supply. For example, introduced plants, such as purple loosestrife or garlic mustard, may outcompete native plants that depend on the same light and space resources. *Predation* refers to the way an animal (predator) feeds on another animal. Rats and snakes are predators of bird species, for example. On the Hawaiian Islands, introduced rats and snakes have caused a number of native bird species to become extinct. *Herbivory* occurs when animals, such as the Asian longhorned beetle, eat plants.

An example of the way invasive species may change ecosystems comes from the southwestern U.S., where the introduced tamarisk tree takes up so much water that it lowers the water table and makes it difficult for the roots of native trees to reach vital groundwater. In the Northeast and Midwest, zebra mussels change aquatic habitats by filtering microscopic particles from the water. This makes the water in lakes and rivers much clearer, affecting which organisms can live there.

WHAT ABOUT *NATIVE* INVASIVE SPECIES?

So far, we have been talking about invasive species that were introduced from other continents. Can you think of any native species that cause problems similar to those caused by introduced, invasive species? White-tailed deer are native to the eastern U.S., but over the last fifty years their populations have skyrocketed in many suburban and rural communities. A recent census in Gettysburg National Park, Pennsylvania, estimated an incredible 447 deer per square mile.

Although most people value deer—they enjoy watching or hunting them—when deer become invasive, they can cause a number of problems. For example, high deer populations cause numerous car accidents and devastate gardens and ornamental plants. Deer also eat tree seedlings and native flowers in forests, thus reducing forest biodiversity.

Are deer populations really too high? Or is it just that because humans are invading deer habitats, we think there are too many deer? It is interesting to note that even in prehistoric times, deer populations most likely did not reach the high levels we see today. Do you have any ideas about how humans might have changed our ecosystems to favor deer? For example, might we have reduced the number of deer predators? Or could we have increased the numbers of plants that deer like to eat?

You can see from the deer example that the problem of invasive species is not limited to plants and animals introduced from abroad. However, the majority of species that become invasive are introduced from other continents. Ecology can help us understand why introduced species are more likely than native species to become invasive. The science of ecology also can help us understand how humans have changed North American ecosystems so that native species, such as deer, are able to reach such high numbers.

CONTROLLING INVASIVE SPECIES

When we think of pollution, we usually think of factories spewing chemicals into the air or toxic spills in rivers and oceans. This is referred to as *chemical pollution*. Ecologists studying invasive species sometimes use the term *biological pollution* to bring attention to the problems caused by these species. Biological pollution is extremely difficult to control. This is because the biological pollutants, or introduced species, reproduce on their own.

A number of methods are used to control invasive plant species. Chemical herbicides can be sprayed. We can pull up individual stems by hand. Some

Some species native to North America, such as the white-tailed deer, become invasive.

species are controlled by mowing. Fire also is used to reduce populations of unwanted species. In the chapters that follow, you will learn about *biological control*, which involves using predators to control invasive species.

Each of these methods has advantages and disadvantages. For example, chemicals may pollute the water and fires may cause air pollution, but these methods generally take less time than pulling by hand. Biological control requires years of research to avoid introducing predators that feed on valuable species but it may be more effective than other methods in the long run. Regardless of what method is used, an understanding of the science of ecology is essential in planning control methods and evaluating their success or failure.

In the next three chapters, we present three different approaches to studying ecology—population, community, and ecosystem. We will use these three branches of ecology to help us understand invasive species in natural areas and how we might control some of the most destructive of these species. Invasive species also are a problem in agricultural lands where they usually are called weeds or pests. However, in this book we focus on invasive species in natural areas, such as wetlands, lakes, and forests, rather than on farms.

It is very difficult to control invasive species once they are present in an ecosystem.

FOR DISCUSSION

▶ What are some invasive species in your area?

▶ What are some of the problems invasive species are causing in your area or elsewhere?

▶ Why do humans value biodiversity?

▶ A number of wildlife species that were once rare are making a comeback. For example, finding groups of up to six white-tailed deer in the middle of suburban yards in Ithaca, New York, is not uncommon. Elk are commonplace and can be seen downtown in smaller cities, such as Banff, in the Rocky Mountains. Coyotes are known to eat pet cats in Portland, Oregon, and other western cities. And mountain lions are a concern to suburban communities in South Dakota, Colorado, and elsewhere. Why might some of these native animals be invading "human territory"? Which is the problem—the wildlife or the humans?

CHAPTER 2

POPULATION ECOLOGY

When a new problem species, such as the zebra mussel or Asian longhorned beetle, is introduced to North America, scientists are concerned with how fast its populations might grow. They are also concerned about where they might spread. Questions about changes in the size and location of populations of organisms and why these changes occur are central to the branch of ecology called *population ecology*. Population ecologists ask

▶ How many individuals of the species are there?

▶ How fast is the population growing or declining and why?

▶ Where are the individuals located?

Population ecology is the study of how populations of organisms change in size and location and why these changes occur.

THE PURPLE LOOSESTRIFE STORY

If you live in the continental U.S., you may have admired purple loosestrife in bloom along roadside ditches in late summer. Huge expanses of purple loosestrife add beauty to North American wetlands during their summer flowering season. Purple loosestrife is also a source of nectar and pollen for bees and it is popular as an ornamental plant in gardens. So why has purple loosestrife been cited by Congress as one of the most destructive introduced plants in North America? And why is it listed as one of "The Dirty Dozen—America's Least Wanted Species" by the prominent conservation organization, The Nature Conservancy?

A group of individuals of a particular species in one area is referred to as a *population*.

Purple loosestrife, also known as the "purple plague," rapidly invades all types of wetlands across the continental U.S. and southern Canada. There, it outcompetes cattails and other native plants. Because animals depend on native plants for food, nesting areas, and shelter, purple loosestrife invasions indirectly harm wildlife. Muskrats, bog turtles, and ducks are some of the species that suffer when purple loosestrife takes over.

FIGURE 1.5
Purple Loosestrife

How did purple loosestrife first arrive in North America?

Purple loosestrife first arrived in North America from Europe in the early 1800s. Similar to many introduced species, it was brought in both accidentally and on purpose. It arrived accidentally as a contaminant of ballast water on ships (similar to how zebra mussels arrived). Gardeners also brought in purple loosestrife as an ornamental plant, and herbalists purposefully introduced it as a treatment for diarrhea, ulcers, and sores.

How did purple loosestrife populations expand over time?

By the 1830s, purple loosestrife was well established along the New England seaboard. The construction of the Erie and other canals in the 1880s allowed purple loosestrife to spread into interior New York and the St. Lawrence River valley. As railroads and roads expanded, purple loosestrife followed. In addition, purple loosestrife plants that were sold as ornamentals and as a source of nectar for honeybees spread into natural wetlands. Over the last two centuries, the "purple plague" has spread to wetlands throughout all the lower 48 states except Florida.

What characteristics of purple loosestrife allow it to expand its populations?

In its native Europe, purple loosestrife is not an invasive plant. It normally makes up only about 5% of the plants in a wetland. Yet, somehow purple loosestrife has been able to expand its populations in North America, outcompeting native plants (Figure 1.6). Species that are successful invaders usually have several of these characteristics:

- They grow rapidly and compete with other plants or animals
- They produce large numbers of seeds at a young age
- Their seeds can survive a long time before sprouting
- Their seeds travel long distances
- They can spread by sprouting from the roots or stems
- They have few predators
- Their native region has a climate similar to that of the U.S.

In North America, purple loosestrife has many of the characteristics typical of an invasive species.

- **Growth.** In the U.S., purple loosestrife grows rapidly, sometimes faster than 1 cm per day. It can grow to 2 m in height. A single plant has 30–50 stems, which shade out other plants. Even though the stems die back in the winter, new stems grow again in the spring from its large root system. Stems also grow back quickly after they are killed by mowing, herbicides, or fire.

FIGURE 1.6
Expansion of Purple Loosestrife in North America

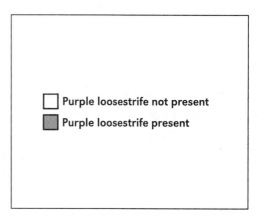

□ Purple loosestrife not present
■ Purple loosestrife present

▶ **Seeds.** Purple loosestrife produces seeds in its first year. A single plant can produce more than 2.5 million seeds annually. The seeds are long lived. They spread easily by floating on water and in mud that sticks to wildlife, livestock, and people's boots. Within a single square meter plot, ecologists have counted up to 20,000 purple loosestrife seedlings.

▶ **Sprouting.** Purple loosestrife develops a large root system that sends up new stems. If a piece of root gets broken off and washed downstream, stems can sprout in a new location.

▶ **Predators.** None of the insects that feed on purple loosestrife in its native Europe occur naturally in North America. Few North American insects feed on purple loosestrife and none are able to control it.

▶ **Native region.** Purple loosestrife is native to Europe and Asia. It occupies regions on these continents that have a climate similar to the regions it occupies in North America.

Ecologists think that these factors have allowed purple loosestrife to expand rapidly across the U.S. Today when scientists help make decisions about whether to introduce a new species, they first ask whether it has characteristics typical of other invasive species. In addition, they determine whether the plant has become invasive when introduced elsewhere.

So far, we have discussed how purple loosestrife spreads to new locations and then expands its numbers. How might population ecology, which focuses on changes in numbers and locations of populations of organisms, help us understand how purple loosestrife becomes invasive?

HOW MANY? ABUNDANCE

Abundance is the number of individuals in a population.

Purple loosestrife becomes a problem when its populations expand in wetlands. We can simply observe that there are a lot of plants, but sometimes it is useful to have a more precise measure of the number of individual stems. Ecologists refer to the number of individuals in a population as its *abundance*. They may want to know if purple loosestrife is becoming more or less abundant each year. Or they may want a good measure of what other species become more abundant after we spray herbicides or otherwise try to control the purple loosestrife.

Density is the number of individuals per unit area.

Density is a measure of the abundance of a plant or animal per unit area. Scientists measure density at different scales, depending on the size of the plant or animal. For plants such as purple loosestrife, density is often measured as number of stems in one square meter. But what about trees? Individual trees may occupy more than one square meter. Forest scientists often measure the number of trees per 0.1 hectare (a hectare is about 2.5 acres). For animals that move, such as deer, wildlife scientists may measure numbers per square kilometer.

SCiLINKS.
THE WORLD'S A CLICK AWAY

Topic: ecology
Go to: www.sciLINKS.org
Code: IE02

Recently, ecologists have been turning their attention to urban areas. Because most of their past work has been in more "natural" settings, ecologists often are ill-prepared to conduct research in highly developed areas like cities. How would you measure plant density in a city? Would you limit your sample to parks and yards or would you include built-up areas? Scientists are trying to answer these questions as they define goals for their research in urban areas.

POPULATION GROWTH

> There is no exception to the rule that every organic being naturally increases at so high a rate that, if not destroyed, the Earth would soon be covered by the progeny of a single pair.
>
> —Charles Darwin, *On the Origin of Species*

Every population has the potential to increase. The rate at which a population can increase depends on its birth rate and the number of females of reproductive age. For example, let's say an animal population starts out with three females able to reproduce, each of whom produces two females per year. In this example, females are capable of reproducing the year they are born and live only one year. To make it simpler, males are not considered.

Table 1.1 shows the growth of this population over a period of 10 years. Figure 1.7 shows the same data in graphical form. You can see that instead of increasing by the same number of individuals each year, the population doubles each year. This is called *exponential growth*.

Topic: population growth
Go to: www.sciLINKS.org
Code: IE04

TABLE 1.1
Exponential Growth in a Population

Year	Number of adult females at beginning of year	Number of females born	Number of adults that die	Total number of individuals at end of year
1	3	6	3	6
2	6	12	6	12
3	12	24	12	24
4	24	48	24	48
5	48	96	48	96
6	96	192	96	192
7	192	384	192	384
8	384	768	384	768
9	768	1536	768	1536
10	1536	3072	1536	3072

FIGURE 1.7
Exponential Growth of a Population

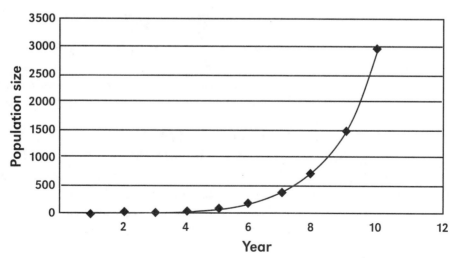

Factors that limit how fast populations of plants and animals can grow include *competition*, *predation*, and *lack of resources*.

Let's assume that the animal whose population is growing exponentially is a snake species that has just been introduced to Hawaii. Would we expect its population to keep growing exponentially for a long period of time? After a while, a number of factors might limit its growth. The snakes themselves might exhaust their existing food resources. Other animals might compete for the same bird eggs that the snake preys on or might prey on the snake itself, or a disease might infest the snakes. Eventually these *limiting factors*, such as lack of resources, competition, predation, and disease, will control the snake population. Together these factors determine the *carrying capacity* or the number of individuals the environment can support.

Thus, the growth of most populations slows down as the density of the population increases. A logistic growth curve demonstrates how growth slows as population density increases (Figure 1.8). Such curves show an increase in a population, followed by a leveling off as the population approaches carrying capacity.

The *carrying capacity* of an ecosystem is the number of individuals of one species the ecosystem can support over a long time period.

Sometimes scientists and land managers try to introduce a new limiting factor to control a rapidly growing population of an invasive species. In the case of purple loosestrife, insects that feed on purple loosestrife are being introduced in an attempt to slow its population growth.

FIGURE 1.8
Logistic Growth of a Population

This graph uses the same data through year 10 as the graph shown in Figure 1.7. However, the scales on the x and y axes are different from those on the first graph.

WHERE? DISTRIBUTION

Maybe you have lots of friends or relatives, but they all live far away so it's hard to visit them. In this case, it's not only how many friends and relatives you have that's important to you but also where they live. Similarly, how organisms are distributed across the landscape, that is, *where* they live, is important to ecologists.

Factors Controlling Distribution

Distribution refers to where a species is located. Three factors control the distribution of a species: colonization, availability of resources and suitable habitat, and interactions with other organisms.

▶ *Colonization.* Colonization refers to a species' first arrival in a new area. How a species colonizes a new area is important in determining its initial distribution. For example, the Asian longhorned beetle arrived accidentally in packing crates in New York City. Thus, the first outbreaks were in New York City and the surrounding areas. Similarly, zebra mussels first entered North America in the Great Lakes and spread from there. The adaptations of a species are important in its ability to colonize new sites. For example, purple loosestrife seeds float on water, allowing them to spread along streams and around lakes and ponds. Asian longhorned beetles are poor flyers, which limits their ability to rapidly spread to new sites.

▶ *Resources and suitable habitat.* The distribution of a species also is controlled by availability of resources and suitable *habitat*. Each species has particular requirements for resources. For plants, these resources include light, water, temperature, and nutrients. Open or unshaded wetland habitats in North America supply the right combination of these resources for purple loosestrife.

Some plants have very specific habitat requirements. For example, the Karner blue butterfly feeds only on lupine plants that grow in the few remaining pine barrens in the eastern and midwestern U.S. (Pine barrens are sandy, open habitats with pine trees, lupines, and other species. Most pine barrens have been destroyed by commercial and residential development.) Because the Karner blue butterfly has such narrow habitat requirements, its distribution is extremely limited. Such rare species with specific habitat requirements are very susceptible to loss of habitat caused by invasive species and other disturbances (e.g., hurricanes or commercial development). In contrast to these rare species, invasive species are often "habitat generalists." They can occupy a broad range of habitats and thus have broad distributions.

▶ *Interactions with other organisms: competition, predation, herbivory.* Finally, some species interact with other species through competition or predation. An individual or species that is able to use resources to grow and reproduce faster than other individuals or species is a superior competitor. A predator is an animal that feeds on another animal, whereas a herbivore is an animal that feeds on a plant. Because purple loosestrife is a superior competitor relative to native wetland plants, it is able to spread in wetlands. The lack of native herbivores also allows purple loosestrife populations to expand.

Distribution refers to **where species are located across the landscape.**

Colonization, availability of resources and habitat, and interactions with other organisms determine a species' distribution.

Habitat refers to the **type of environment in which a species occurs and includes physical and biological conditions.**

Distribution and Control of Invasive Species

How can knowing the distribution of an invasive species help in its control? One of the most important findings guiding management of invasive species has to do with distribution patterns. Using computer models of population growth, scientists have determined that several small populations of invasive species spread more rapidly than one large population. Why might this be so?

Consider three small patches of purple loosestrife and assume that each is in the shape of a circle (Figure 1.9). Now consider one large circular patch of purple loosestrife (Figure 1.10). Let's assume that the total area of all three smaller patches combined is equal to the area of the large patch.

But what about their circumferences? The circumference is important because it is the outside of the patch—the part right next to the area of the wetland that is not yet colonized by purple loosestrife. If you add together the three circumferences of the smaller patches, the number you get is larger than the circumference of the one larger patch. Thus, more seeds are likely to land outside the three small patches than outside the one large patch. In the larger patch, many seeds may land within the patch itself.

FIGURE 1.9
Area and Circumference of Three Small Patches

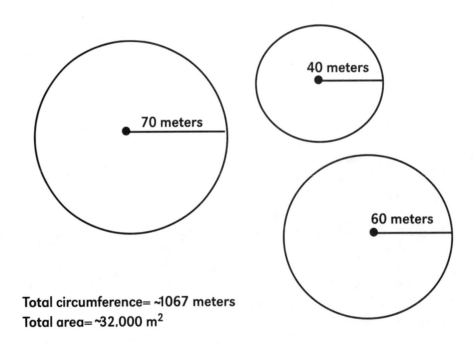

70 meters

40 meters

60 meters

Total circumference= ~1067 meters
Total area= ~32,000 m^2

FIGURE 1.10
Area and Circumference of One Large Patch

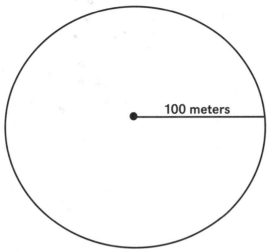

Circumference=~628 meters
Area=~32,000 m^2

If you had to choose between spending time and money to destroy a large patch of an invasive species or several small patches, your efforts would be best spent destroying the small populations. Once a species has spread to form a large patch, it already will have impacted the local habitat and often will be extremely difficult to control. Removing a few plants is much easier and still destroys plants that may provide seeds for new populations. Thus, it is essential to locate and eradicate small populations of problem invasive species before they expand.

Scientists, Environmentalists, and Policy Makers

Many citizens and people in power want to do something to help our environment. Science can help these environmentalists and policy makers target their actions so that they are most effective.

Regulators deciding what new plants should be allowed into the U.S. take into account what we know about invasive species. For example, it is advisable to avoid plants that have become invasive elsewhere, that grow in climates similar to those of North America, that produce large number of seeds, and that have no known predators or herbivores in North America.

Even so, ecologists still cannot reliably predict what will happen when a new species is introduced into North America. This inability to predict what will happen when humans change the environment in some way is common. This happens because we lack a complete understanding of ecology and other sciences. However, often scientists can help environmentalists and policy makers make the best possible predictions, and then these groups can work together to monitor the results of any actions taken.

FOR DISCUSSION

▶ You are working for the U.S. Department of Agriculture and get a request from a nursery company to bring a new species into the U.S. for use as an ornamental plant. What questions might you ask about this species if you wanted to determine whether it was likely to become invasive?

▶ You have just discovered a small patch of the invasive plant garlic mustard in a local forest. Assuming nothing is done to control the garlic mustard, draw a diagram of the population curve you might expect for garlic mustard in this forest over the next five years. Now draw a curve for the next thirty years assuming no control measures are taken. Again assuming nothing is done to control the garlic mustard, draw population curves for the next five and next thirty years for native species that are already in the forest, such as trilliums, jack-in-the-pulpit, toothwort, and spring beauty.

▶ You and your classmates are conducting a survey to find out the distribution of a non-native, invasive plant that colonizes wetlands and has just entered your county. Draw a diagram or a map of what you would expect its distribution to be. Now, assume the species has been in your county for twenty years, and no one has tried to control it. How does its distribution differ from when it first entered the county? Draw a map of how you think the plant would be distributed in the county if no control measures were taken. How would its distribution be different if control measures had been taken when it first entered the county?

CHAPTER 3

COMMUNITY ECOLOGY

Whereas population ecologists are concerned about numbers and distributions of individuals and species, community ecologists study how different individuals and species interact. Community ecologists ask questions such as

▶ What happens when species feed on other species?

▶ How do individuals and species compete with each other?

▶ How do communities of plants and animals change over time?

▶ How do disturbances, such as hurricanes, oil spills, or invasions of introduced species, affect plant and animal communities?

Community ecology is the study of how different organisms and species interact through processes such as predation and competition.

WHO FEEDS ON WHOM?

Predators, Herbivores, Parasites, and Pathogens

When we think of predators, we usually think of large fish, mammals, or birds feeding on smaller or weaker animals. Sharks prey on fish, wolves prey on young moose, and eagles prey on salmon. But insect predators are far more numerous than large animal predators. Insects feed on other species of insects and occasionally on vertebrates such as frogs and mammals. Many insects also feed on plants and are called *herbivores*.

Herbivores are animals that eat plants. Many herbivores are insects.

The gypsy moth is an introduced herbivore that feeds on the leaves of forest trees. It was introduced to North America from China on purpose—people wanted to use it to make silk, like the Chinese silkworm. It was unsuccessful as a silk producer but has become a significant pest, contributing to the death of many thousands of acres of hardwood forests in North America. Gypsy moths are invasive, but their populations vary from one year to the next and they generally don't kill all the trees in a forest.

We often think about insects that damage trees and other plants important to humans. But insects and other herbivores also can help keep plant populations under control. By keeping the population of any one species in check, herbivores sometimes enhance biodiversity. For example, in Europe many herbivores feed on purple loosestrife, which undoubtedly helps control purple loosestrife populations. This is one reason why purple loosestrife constitutes only about 5% of the plants in European wetlands, rather than dominating wetlands as it does in North America. By keeping the population of any one species low, insects and other herbivores allow a diversity of species to coexist.

Scientists and land managers sometimes take advantage of the ability of herbivores and predators to control populations of problem species. This purposeful introduction of insects or other organisms to control unwanted species is called *biological control*. Organisms used in biological control are tested to make sure they only prey or feed on the problem species. Bringing in such "specialist" organisms reduces the chance that they will harm native species.

The purposeful introduction of specialized insects or other organisms to control unwanted species is called *biological control*.

In addition to predators and herbivores, parasites and pathogens can cause problems and can help control pest species. Parasites and pathogens include bacteria, viruses, fungi, and other small organisms. Parasites feed on live plants or animals but generally do not kill them, whereas pathogens kill their host plant or animal. Just as native plants may not have resistance to a newly introduced herbivore, they may not be resistant to attack by an introduced fungus or microbe. Additionally, there may not be any natural controls of the newly introduced fungus or microorganism. The result is that even tiny microorganisms, like the chestnut blight fungus discussed in Chapter 1, can kill large trees and other organisms and can decimate entire species.

Similar to predators and herbivores, parasites and pathogens can be used to control unwanted organisms. Currently, scientists are researching the effectiveness of a virus that attacks gypsy moth caterpillars, in the hope of developing a biological control for this problem insect.

Biological Control: Applying Our Understanding of Population and Community Ecology

Although purple loosestrife was first brought to the U.S. as a medicinal and garden plant, people became concerned when it started to invade wetlands. Early efforts to control purple loosestrife were unsuccessful. The "purple plague" was able to grow back after repeatedly being cut, burned, mowed, treated with herbicides, and flooded, and after repeated attempts to create dry conditions by lowering the water level.

Because these methods of control were unsuccessful, scientists turned to biological control. Biological control involves using natural enemies of an undesired species to reduce its populations. These natural enemies may be herbivores, predators, or parasites, such as viruses and bacteria. They often are introduced from the plant or animal's native region. For example, insects from Europe are brought to North America to control purple loosestrife. Biological control does not completely wipe out a species. However, it can reduce populations of invasive species so that their threat to desirable organisms is greatly reduced or minimal.

Scientists disagree about whether biological control is a good way to control purple loosestrife and other non-native pest species. Thinking back to what you know about the purple loosestrife problem in North America and about biological control, can you suggest why there is this controversy among scientists? Is introducing one non-native species to control another non-native species a good practice?

Scientific Disagreement

Many questions in science are very difficult to answer. It often takes researchers using different methods over many years to find a satisfactory answer. For example, ecologists studying the effect of global warming on plants may use computer models, studies of plant distribution, and controlled laboratory experiments. During the time when this research is going on, it is not surprising that scientists, especially those using different approaches, often disagree.

In many cases, scientists disagree on smaller points but are in general agreement on larger issues. For example, the overwhelming majority of scientists now agree that global warming is occurring. Yet they may disagree on how fast global warming is occurring and its effects on ecosystems.

Disagreement among scientists has both negative and positive consequences. On the negative side, strong disagreements may hinder productive debate and thus prevent scientists from working toward a common understanding. Also, politicians and the media often pick up on scientific disagreement and may use the results of a small group of scientists to back a particular point of view. An often-used argument by politicians and the media when discussing public policy is that "even scientists don't agree." This statement may be used to exaggerate the degree of disagreement among scientists and to suggest that disagreement proves the scientists have failed.

Disagreement also can be a positive force in science. It often sparks productive debate among scientists, leading to creative new ideas and solutions. It encourages others to join in the search for answers to scientific questions. Healthy disagreement followed by meaningful discussion keeps scientists thinking about the meaning of their results, instead of just settling on the first answer that comes to mind.

Scientists who argue against biological control point out past problems where one species was brought in to control another introduced species. In early cases of biological control, the cure sometimes proved worse than the original problem. For example, by the late 1700s, rats introduced to Jamaica from Europe already had become a problem. A Jamaican sugar planter introduced an aggressive Cuban ant in the hopes that it would kill the rats. The ants were unsuccessful in controlling the rats but their populations grew rapidly and they themselves became a problem. A huge South American toad was next introduced to control the rats and the ants. It too was unsuccessful as a biological control agent but it became established and infested sugar plantations. So a mongoose was introduced from India to control the rats. Within thirty years after its arrival in Jamaica, the mongoose had destroyed native bird and reptile populations.

However, the science of biological control has progressed way beyond initial ill-fated attempts like the one in Jamaica. We now have a number of biological control success stories, largely because scientists better understand the effect of herbivores on plants. The biological control of Klamath weed in California and the prickly pear cactus in Australia are examples of success stories. Klamath weed was brought into California from Europe in the early 1900s and by 1944 had spread over two million acres of rangeland. Similarly, when prickly pear was introduced from South America to Australia, it quickly invaded thousands of acres of valuable rangeland and pasture. Because Klamath weed is poisonous, and the prickly pear cactus is inedible to livestock, control of these species was a high priority. In both cases, insects introduced to control these species dramatically reduced their populations. Within less than ten years, the Klamath weed and prickly pear cactus were no longer pests of rangelands.

Host-specific organisms feed on only one or a very few species. Modern biological control efforts use host-specific insects and microorganisms.

Unlike mongooses and rats, which are generalists and feed on a variety of species, insects used in modern biological control of plants are specialists, or *host-specific*—they feed only on the target invasive plant species. Thus, they are able to control the pest species without threatening valued agricultural and native species.

Steps in Biological Control of Plants Using Insects

How do scientists find such host-specific insects to use for biological control? A typical biological control program, such as that for purple loosestrife, follows these steps.

1. *Identify insects that are feeding on the introduced plant where it has been introduced.* If insects already present in North America are good controls for the plant, scientists will save a lot of time and money by not having to follow the lengthy process needed to get approval to introduce non-native insects.

2. *Identify host-specific insects in the target plant's native region.* A successful biological control insect should be host-specific— that is, it should feed and reproduce only on the target pest species (e.g., purple loosestrife) and not on other plants.

3. *Test effects of insects on growth of target plant.*

4. *Select insects that have broad geographic distribution and dramatic impact on the growth of the target species.* It is important that the insect have a broad distribution so it will control the target species over a large area.

5. *Identify test plants.* Test plants are species that may be at risk of attack by the insects because they are closely related to the target species, grow in the same habitat as the target species, or are important ecologically or economically (e.g., species important in agriculture).

6. *Test for host specificity.* Test to see if the insects that were selected feed on the test plants or only on the target plant.

7. *Seek government approval.* A board of biological control experts in the U.S. and Canada reviews the studies and grants permission to introduce the biocontrol insects.

8. *Test potential for biological control.* Studies are conducted to determine whether the biocontrol insects are likely themselves to be eaten by predators. If it appears that the biocontrol insects will survive in the wild, studies are conducted to develop ways to rear them.

9. *Release and monitor.* Scientists release the biocontrol insects and then conduct research to answer questions such as: How many insects are needed to control different-sized populations of the target species? What is the best time of year to release the biocontrol organism?

10. *Evaluate effectiveness.* Monitor the target species to see if its populations are being reduced.

11. *Long-term monitoring.* Follow-up studies are conducted to determine the long-term effect of the biocontrol insects, including what plants take over after the target species dies. This is especially important because often management actions must be taken to ensure that a desirable species, rather than another invasive species, replaces the species that has been controlled.

Each step in this process reduces the possibility of something going wrong (e.g., the insects attacking a native plant in North America) and increases the probability of controlling the target species.

However, even the scientists most involved in the biocontrol of a species, such as purple loosestrife, cannot be absolutely sure that the introduced insects will never become a pest of native or commercially valuable plants in North America. But they can help us weigh the benefits and risks of biological control. We know that in the absence of biological control of purple loosestrife, native plants and wildlife in wetlands will suffer. Based on our understanding of entomology, plant biology, and ecology, we know it is extremely unlikely that the biocontrol insects will threaten any species other than purple loosestrife. With this knowledge in hand, the U.S. and Canadian governments decided the real risks of purple loosestrife outweighed any potential risks of introducing the control insects. So far, their decision seems to have been a wise one.

In Michigan and New York State, citizen groups and schools are raising the beetles used in biological control of purple loosestrife. They also monitor the populations of purple loosestrife and other wetland plants before and after releasing the insects. Similar to scientists and land managers, these students and volunteers are applying their understanding of ecology to managing our environment. Instructions for raising and releasing biological control beetles and monitoring their impacts on purple loosestrife are included in Section 3 of this book.

Uncertainty in Science

Policy makers need to make decisions based on scientific information. But as we have seen in the purple loosestrife biological control research, scientists often are not 100% sure about outcomes. This uncertainty is common in ecology for several reasons.

First, ecology is a relatively new science, just over hundred years old, and thus ecologists are still developing many of the principles that guide their science. For example, ecologists still are conducting experiments and constructing computer models to help us understand competition. In addition, results scientists get in the lab, where they can control conditions, often do not predict exactly what will happen in nature, where weather and other factors vary. Finally, researchers often are able to conduct research only for a short period, whereas they are trying to predict what might happen over decades.

FOOD CHAINS AND FOOD WEBS

A *food chain* shows the feeding relationships among plants and animals in an ecosystem.

Animals and the plants they feed on are linked together in food chains and food webs. A *food chain* is a sequence of feeding relationships that begins with a plant, which is in turn eaten by an animal, which is in turn eaten by another animal (Figure 1.11).

A green plant that gets energy directly from the Sun and thus does not depend on energy from other organisms is called a *primary producer*. The word "primary" is used because green plants that produce sugars using energy from the Sun are at the first level in the food chain. An animal feeding directly on a plant is called a *primary consumer*. An animal feeding on the primary consumer is called a *secondary consumer*.

FIGURE 1.11
Example of a Food Chain

Tertiary consumer

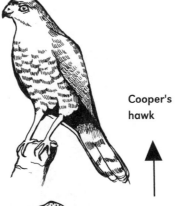

Cooper's hawk

Secondary consumer

European starling

Primary consumers eat plants, and *secondary consumers* eat animals that feed on plants.

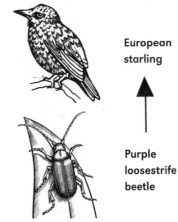

Primary consumer

Purple loosestrife beetle

Primary producer

Purple loosestrife

Primary producers are green plants, which get their energy directly from the Sun.

Food webs show the relationships between multiple primary producers and consumers.

Food webs are similar to food chains, except that they have several primary producers and primary and secondary consumers. Food webs more accurately reflect the complex interactions that occur in nature (Figure 1.12).

FIGURE 1.12
Example of a Food Web

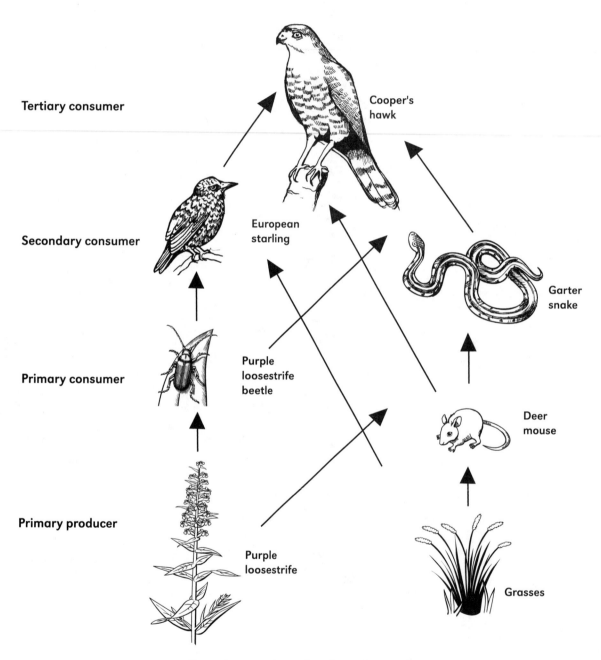

Tertiary consumer — Cooper's hawk

Secondary consumer — European starling / Garter snake

Primary consumer — Purple loosestrife beetle / Deer mouse

Primary producer — Purple loosestrife / Grasses

Sometimes an introduced species can have an impact on an entire food web (Figures 1.13 and 1.14). In the 1960s and 1970s, the state of Montana was searching for a way to increase salmon populations for fishermen. They introduced the opossum shrimp as a source of food for the fish. Unfortunately, the shrimp proved to be a hungry predator of copepods, which are microorganisms that the young salmon had been feeding on. Salmon populations declined drastically. So did many animals that preyed on the salmon, including eagles, gulls, otters, coyotes, and bears. Thus, introducing a small animal low in the food web caused an impact on numerous consumers and changed the entire community of organisms.

FIGURE 1.13
Salmon Food Web

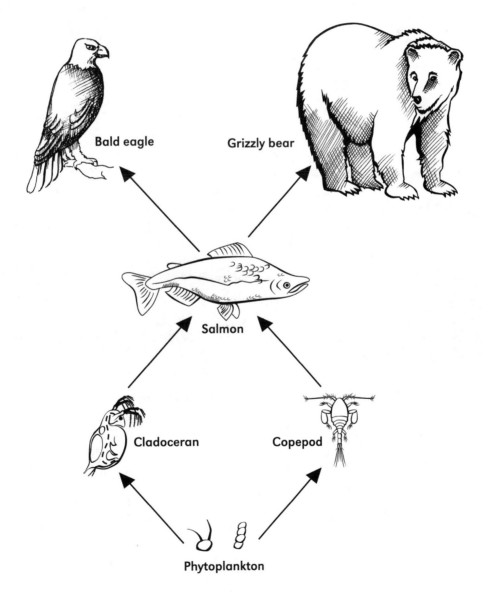

Before the introduction of opossum shrimp, bald eagles and grizzly bears fed on salmon, whose main food source was copepods and other microorganisms.

FIGURE 1.14
Collapse of the Salmon Food Web

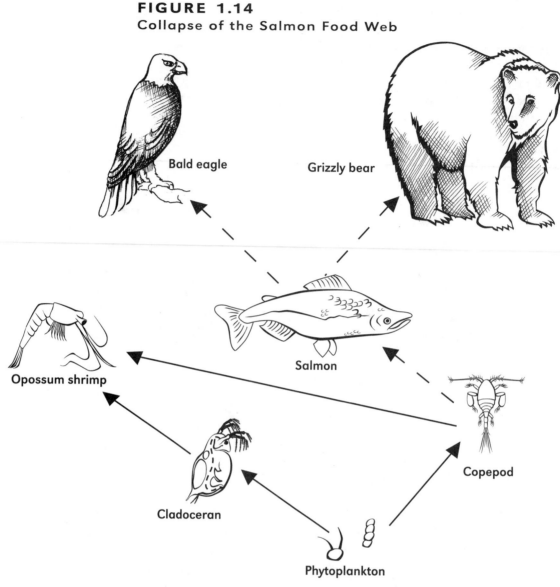

Introduced opossum shrimp fed heavily on the copepods, thereby causing a decline in salmon populations. This in turn resulted in declines in the populations of eagles and bears that fed on the salmon. Solid arrows indicate new food web after opossum shrimp were introduced. Dotted arrows indicate links in food web that changed after opossum shrimp were introduced.

COMPETITION

Like predation, *competition* affects the abundance and distribution of individuals and species. When two or more individuals compete, the result is reduced growth of one of the individuals. When two or more species compete, the result is a reduced population of one species. Competition can be for both physical and biological resources. For example, plants may compete for sunlight, soil nutrients, water, space, and pollinators. Animals may compete for food, mates, and space or territories.

Predation and herbivory are easy to observe—we can actually see an insect eat another insect or a plant. In contrast, it is extremely difficult to observe the process of competition. How can we be sure that organisms really do compete?

Experiments with aquatic microorganisms provide evidence that competition actually occurs (Figure 1.15). In the 1980s, ecologist David Tilman grew two species of microorganisms called diatoms in a flask. Both diatom species require silica for growth. He grew each species alone with added silica, and they each showed logistic population growth (see Chapter 2, p. 18). He also noted that one species used more silica than the other. When the two species were grown together, species 1, which used more silica, drove species 2 to extinction within the flask. Thus, the first species was a superior competitor for silica.

Competition **between two individuals or species results in reduced growth of one of the individuals or a reduced population of one of the species.**

FIGURE 1.15
Microcosm Experiment Demonstrating Competition between Aquatic Microorganisms

When the two species of microorganisms were grown separately, they each showed a logistic population growth curve. When the two species were grown together, the species that used more silica (species 1) drove species 2 to extinction within the flask.

Dr. Tilman's experiment in flasks is an example of a *microcosm experiment*. In microcosm experiments, scientists grow organisms in a mini-ecosystem, such as a glass jar or flask. They are able to keep constant or control factors that may influence their results, such as the amount of food, temperature, light, and space. By controlling these factors, the scientists are fairly certain that the factor they vary—for example, silica— is responsible for their results. However, microcosm studies have been criticized for creating artificial conditions that may not reflect what occurs in nature. Therefore, there is always a question of whether the results from a microcosm experiment can really predict what would happen under more natural conditions.

Even though scientists are aware of the limitations of microcosm experiments, they cannot simply replace such experiments with ones under more natural conditions. This is because it is much more difficult to design a competition or other experiment in the field, where factors in addition to those that you are measuring may influence your results. For example, if you wanted to test whether two plant species competed with each other in the field, you would need to consider questions such as: Do factors such as sunlight or soil moisture vary between the sites where the different species are growing? Will my experiment be destroyed if we encounter unusual weather (e.g., drought or floods) or herbivores during the growing season? How will I measure the effect of competition?

Because competition experiments are difficult to conduct under natural conditions, there are few examples of controlled field experiments that demonstrate competition. Instead, scientists often use careful *observations* of what is occurring in nature as circumstantial evidence, but not proof, of competition. For instance, when zebra mussels were introduced into the Great Lakes, the populations of native mussels declined greatly. Similarly, when purple loosestrife invades wetlands, the populations of cattails and other native plants decrease. These observations do not prove that competition is occurring between the introduced and native species, or even that the zebra mussels or purple loosestrife caused the declines in the other species. To prove that the invasive species are the true culprits, the observations must be backed up by additional observations and experiments.

DISTURBANCE AND SUCCESSION

A *community of organisms* refers to the plants and animals present in an ecosystem, such as a forest or lake.

Populations of organisms within a community are constantly changing. Ongoing predation and competition may change what species are present or abundant. Disturbances often cause larger changes in species composition. Changes in the availability of resources, such as light and nitrogen, are often the result of disturbances and also can impact species composition. Most people think of "disturbances" as physical events such as fire, floods, volcanic eruptions, or the clear-cutting of forests. However, disturbances also can be biological, such as the introduction of an invasive species. For example, purple loosestrife and zebra mussels cause major disturbances to plant and animal communities.

Following a major disturbance, such as a fire or volcanic eruption, plants will recolonize the disturbed site. In the northeastern U.S., a recently disturbed site is generally colonized by herbaceous species (plants that do not have wood), such as grasses and goldenrod. Eventually shrubs will become established on the site, followed by trees. As trees die, changes will continue to occur. This process of change in species over time is called *succession*. The grasses and goldenrod are early successional species, shrubs and trees that grow in open areas are mid-successional species, and trees that grow in shaded areas are late successional species.

Disturbances such as fires, floods, clear-cutting, and the introduction of invasive species change plant and animal communities.

FIGURE 1.16
The Succession of Species

Early succession - - - - - - - - - - - - - → Late succession

Grasses   Shrubs   Trees

Humans cause many disturbances to ecosystems. For example, when humans build roads, roadsides first are disturbed by construction equipment and later are repeatedly disturbed by mowing and spraying herbicides. By repeatedly disturbing a site, the process of succession is disrupted. In a park or yard that is mowed throughout the summer, only early successional herbaceous species, such as grass, are able to survive. Similarly, many introduced species are early successional and thrive on disturbed sites. For example, Japanese bamboo, garlic mustard, and white sweet clover (all introduced species) do well on disturbed sites and often are abundant along disturbed roadsides.

Succession **is the process of change in plant and animal communities over time.**

On sites that are left undisturbed, early successional species are replaced by middle and then late successional species. For example, in northeastern forests, early successional asters are replaced by pin cherry trees, which are replaced by maple, beech, spruce, and fir trees. Late successional plant and animal communities are referred to as *climax communities*.

For many years, ecologists held to the *equilibrium theory*. This theory stated that ecosystems move toward a climax community of plants and animals, with practically no further changes in species. However, during the 1980s and 1990s, research showed that disturbance and change in plant and animal communities occur continually. Thus, ecological communities generally do not reach a fixed composition of plants and animals without further changes. Instead, changes in species abundances and distributions are an ongoing process. Contemporary ecologists like to talk about the *flux* of nature rather than the *balance* of nature. That is, ecologists now realize that even in late successional communities, plant and animal populations still change. This is one of many examples of how scientific understanding changes as a result of new research findings.

Scientific Understandings Change as New Discoveries Are Made

The change in the way ecologists view succession is just one example of how scientists' understanding of nature changes as new evidence is presented. For many years, ecologists believed late successional communities were stable—that species did not change until a new disturbance, such as a hurricane, wiped out the existing plants.

As new evidence accumulated, scientists came to realize that even late successional communities constantly undergo changes, as individual trees die from disease or are toppled over by wind, and new species become established. Thus, the idea of a stable, climax community is no longer widely accepted in ecology. New research continuously adds to our understanding of nature.

WHITE-TAILED DEER: APPLYING OUR UNDERSTANDING OF POPULATION AND COMMUNITY ECOLOGY

In the early 1900s, white-tailed deer were dangerously near extinction in many parts of their range. Unregulated hunting had reduced the number of deer to 500,000 in the entire U.S. To address the problem of deer and other declining wildlife populations, states formed wildlife agencies. Their goal was to conserve the nation's depleted wildlife resources.

The wildlife agencies prohibited the harvesting of female deer, thus allowing reproduction rates to increase. At the same time, predators of deer, such as wolves and mountain lions, were eliminated from many places by hunting. This removed one of the factors limiting the populations of deer. More recently, habitat changes have encouraged growth of deer populations. For example, in much of the northeastern U.S., abandoned farms are growing back to forests, and people are moving into suburban and rural areas. These trends have created a mix of open fields, lawns, gardens, and forests, which are ideal for deer. Furthermore, many rural landowners are posting their land against hunting, and hunting is prohibited in suburban and urban communities. Thus, through an increase in suitable habitat and a decrease in animal and human predation, deer populations are no longer kept in check.

Today there are over twenty million deer in the U.S. and populations are increasing. Densities exceed forty deer per square mile in some rural areas, and over four hundred deer per square mile have been documented. Is the resulting rebound of white-tailed deer populations a wildlife management success or a terrible failure? This probably depends on whom you talk to!

Many people enjoy hunting deer, while others enjoy watching them. However, as the number of deer increases, public attitudes become more negative. Deer cause damage to crops, gardens, and ornamental plants. Deer also eat plants in the forest, harming seedlings of valuable species such as sugar maple and oaks. By eating small trees and shrubs, deer destroy important habitats for many insects and birds. Deer also can be a hazard to humans. Car collisions with deer are common in many areas of North America, and deer carry Lyme disease, which causes symptoms similar to flu and arthritis, and if not treated, can be fatal.

Unlike purple loosestrife and zebra mussels, white-tailed deer are native to North America. However, deer are similar in many ways to introduced, invasive species. Neither purple loosestrife nor deer have predators that are able to keep their populations in check. Both species can be a major disturbance to an ecosystem, through outcompeting native plants in the case of purple loosestrife, or feeding on native plants in the case of deer. Once the native plants are gone, the populations of animals that depend on them also will decline, resulting in a loss of biodiversity.

In suburban Cayuga Heights, New York, citizens are contributing to a study of deer in their community. They record their observations of deer, such as the number of males and females, and what the deer are eating. They then fill out forms on the Web and submit their data to Cornell University wildlife biologists. Together, the scientists and community members are coming up with recommendations for how to manage deer populations in this suburban neighborhood.

Students and other citizens in New York State also are contributing to studies of the effect of deer on the regeneration of plants. They construct small deer *exclosures* using fences. The fences keep deer out of the study plots. Nearby *control* or *reference plots* are set up in areas to which deer have access. The scientists and citizens then conduct vegetation surveys to determine the effect of deer on plants.

Citizens Contribute to Scientific Research

The suburban deer study is just one example of how citizens and students have contributed to scientific studies. Currently, there are a number of opportunities for students to help scientists collect data and form "student/scientist partnerships." You may have heard of the GLOBE project, in which students from around the world collect data on local temperature, rainfall, and other factors, in an effort to help scientists understand climate and environmental change. The Cornell Laboratory of Ornithology offers opportunities for students to collect information on birds visiting their feeders. The students' data help scientists understand changes in bird populations.

Similarly, youth in cities across North America are working with the Cornell Department of Natural Resources to collect data on urban community gardens. We have included two examples of students working with scientists to collect data on invasive species in Section 3; one example focuses on common reed (*Phragmites*) and the other on purple loosestrife.

Why might scientists want students and citizens to contribute data to their studies? Imagine you are a scientist studying invasive species at Cornell University. You want to develop a biological control program for an invasive species. There may be some insects that already are helping to control this species, but finding them is like finding a needle in a haystack. You don't have the funds to travel across North America looking for the tiny insect larvae. On the other hand, if students across North America could each survey the insects on this plant in their area and then send you their data, you might have the problem solved. Thus, one reason scientists involve students in their research is that they need to collect data over a large geographic area but don't have the time or the money to collect the data themselves.

Another reason scientists involve citizens and students in their research is that they want to educate people about science. They believe that through participating in a real research project, students will better learn about science and what it takes to become a scientist.

COMMUNITY ECOLOGY, POPULATION ECOLOGY, AND INVASIVE SPECIES

Understanding concepts in community and population ecology can help us manage invasive species. In Chapter 2, you learned that patterns of distribution are important in predicting what might happen when invasive species spread to other habitats. You learned that plants with very specific habitat requirements, such as the Karner blue butterfly, are likely to be affected by disturbance, including a disturbance caused by invasive species.

Understanding competition and predation also can help us to predict which organisms and habitats are likely to be affected by introduced species. For example, because many islands are isolated, species on islands often have evolved in the presence of very few competitors and predators. Potential competitors and predators are not able to colonize islands because they can't swim or fly to such distant places.

When humans introduce a new species to an island, it may wreak havoc on native plants and animals that have evolved without any defenses to the introduced species. For example, birds native to Guam, an island about six thousand miles west of California, have evolved in the absence of most predators. As a result, these birds do not have defensive behaviors common to birds that evolved in areas where predators, such as snakes, are present. In the 1940s, the brown tree snake was accidentally introduced to Guam, and native bird populations began to plummet. Most birds native to Guam are diurnal (awake during the day). The snakes, which hunt at night, easily find and kill the sleeping birds. The snakes' success has allowed them to reproduce quickly, which has resulted in the death of even more birds. Today at least eight species of birds native to Guam have become extinct, all due to the introduction of the non-native, brown tree snake. Efforts are currently underway to keep the brown tree snake from entering other islands such as Hawaii (e.g., as a "stowaway" on an airplane), where birds could face similar fates.

In fact, staggering numbers of animal and plant species native to Hawaii already have gone extinct. Predators such as rats and mongooses, which were brought to Hawaii by humans, have decimated many bird populations. Competition from non-native species also has had an effect. For example, at least 160 species of alien birds have been introduced to the islands of Hawaii, and at least fifty of those have established breeding populations. Some of these species are able to outcompete native birds for resources such as space and food. About 75% of all plant and animal extinctions in the entire U.S. have occurred in Hawaii. Almost all of these were affected by competition and predation from introduced species.

FOR DISCUSSION

▶ There has been a heated debate among ecologists about biological control. Some think it is wrong to introduce a new species to control a previously introduced species that has become invasive. They fear the control species may itself become invasive and cause more problems than the species it was introduced to control. To support this point of view, these scientists cite examples of where biological control has failed. Other scientists say that with the safeguards now required in biological control programs, it is extremely unlikely that an insect or other species introduced to control an invasive species will cause a problem. These scientists say we need to weigh this very tiny risk of a problem against the benefits of controlling unwanted invasive species.

What do you think are the pros and cons of using biological control for invasive species? How does biological control compare with other possible management options (e.g., applying herbicides, pulling up plants by hand, or burning)?

▶ Learn about an invasive species following the directions for the **Invasive Species Profile** exercise below. Then discuss with your classmates the following questions about the species you have investigated.

a. How have invasive species impacted food webs? Diagram the food web of the communities that have been invaded by the species you investigated, both before and after the species invaded.

b. List the habitats along with the invasive species present in each. What types of habitats appear to be vulnerable to invasive species?

c. Do the communities where invasive species are found tend to be early or late successional communities? What kinds of disturbances, in addition to invasive species, have impacted these communities?

SCI
LINKS.
THE WORLD'S A CLICK AWAY

Topic: invasive species
Go to: www.sciLINKS.org
Code: IE01

INVASIVE SPECIES PROFILE

Choose an invasive species that interests you and answer the questions below. You may want to use the Internet as there are some excellent invasive species websites. However, in order to avoid biased or inaccurate information, be careful in choosing Internet sites—they should be from government agencies, universities, or reputable conservation organizations with scientists on their staffs (such as The Nature Conservancy).

1. Name of species

2. What continent or country did the species come from?

3. How was it introduced to North America? Was it introduced accidentally or on purpose?

4. When and where was it introduced?

5. What is its current distribution in North America? (You can draw a map or describe the region of North America where it is present.)

6. What conditions allowed the species to spread (e.g., lack of predators, favorable habitat)?

7. What characteristics of the organism allow it to invade natural habitat and displace native species?

8. What habitats does it occupy? Are these habitats disturbed (e.g., by road construction) or mostly undisturbed?

9. What are its predators in its native country? Does anything prey on it in the U.S.?

10. If the species is an animal, what plants or other animals does it feed on?

11. If the species is a microorganism that causes disease, what species does it affect?

12. Does it seem to outcompete native or other non-native species where it is invading? Please explain.

13. What problems is it causing in North America?

14. What means, if any, are being used to control the species (biological, chemical, pulling)? Are they effective?

15. Are there any local efforts for monitoring the population of the species? For controlling the species? Are there opportunities for students and volunteers to join in these efforts? Please describe.

CHAPTER 4

ECOSYSTEM ECOLOGY

> Some invaders don't merely compete with or consume native species. By altering environmental conditions or resource availability, they threaten native species by changing the rules of the game.
>
> —*Peter Vitousek, ecologist at Stanford University*

S o far, you have learned how populations, or groups of organisms of the same species, change over time. You also have learned about how communities of organisms of different species interact through competition and predation. In this chapter, we will build on this understanding of population and community ecology to learn how communities of organisms interact with the *abiotic* (nonliving) factors in their environments, such as water and nutrients. The study of the cycling of energy and nutrients between organisms and the abiotic environment is the main focus of ecosystem ecology.

Ecosystem ecology **is the study of the cycling of energy and nutrients between organisms and the nonliving environment.**

You may have studied how individual plants capture the Sun's energy in a process called photosynthesis. Using the Sun's energy, plants are able to make sugars from carbon dioxide (CO_2) present in the atmosphere and water taken up from the soil. *Primary production* refers to the rate at which green plants and some microorganisms are able to convert CO_2 to sugar using the Sun's energy. Different ecosystems have varying rates of primary production, depending on temperature, moisture, the availability of nutrients and sunlight, and other factors. Because all life, including human, depends on the primary producers, the rate of primary production in different ecosystems is an important research topic for ecosystem scientists.

ENERGY FLOW IN ECOSYSTEMS

The sugars produced by photosynthesis become the source of energy for plants, for the animals that eat them, and eventually for the entire food web. Ecosystem scientists are concerned with how this energy moves from the producers (plants and microorganisms) to consumers (animals) and eventually to the microorganisms, fungi, and invertebrates that decompose dead plants and animals.

Trophic levels **help us understand how energy moves from primary producers to consumers in a food web.**

Both community ecologists and ecosystem ecologists describe the relationships of organisms in an ecosystem to each other. As you saw in Chapter 3, community ecologists look at what species are feeding on each other and use food webs to represent these predator/prey relationships. Ecosystem scientists categorize organisms in food webs into different *trophic levels* (see Figure 1.17).

Trophic levels reflect how energy is transformed as one moves from primary producers to consumers and decomposers. Plants, or primary producers, occupy the first trophic level because they directly convert the Sun's energy into sugars. These sugars, or carbon compounds, are incorporated into the plant's tissues. Herbivores derive energy from the primary producers when they feed on them. Herbivores occupy the second trophic level. Carnivores that feed on herbivores occupy the third level, and predators feeding on carnivores occupy the fourth level. Decomposers are somewhat harder to place on a single trophic level because they feed on and thus derive energy from dead plants, dead herbivores, and dead carnivores. Herbivores, carnivores, and decomposers, like primary producers, serve an essential role in the transformation of energy and cycling of nutrients.

FIGURE 1.17
Energy Transfer through Three Trophic Levels

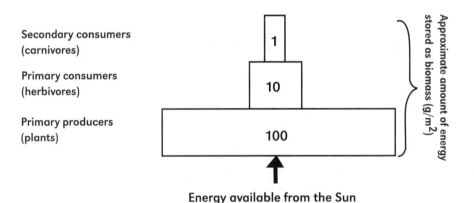

Primary producers convert energy received from sunlight into plant tissue or *biomass*. Biomass is measured in grams of plant tissue per square meter of forest or other ecosystem. Primary consumers feed on and obtain energy from primary producers but convert only about 10% into their own biomass (the rest is lost as heat). Secondary consumers feed on primary consumers, again converting only about 10% of the energy obtained into their own biomass.

THE CARBON CYCLE

As it moves from primary producers to consumers and decomposers, carbon cycles between living organisms and the nonliving environment. In this cycle, compounds that contain chains of carbon and hydrogen atoms are referred to as *organic compounds,* and others are known as *inorganic compounds.*

Through the process of photosynthesis, plants take up inorganic CO_2 from the atmosphere and convert it to organic sugars. Plants and microorganisms that live in water also carry out photosynthesis, taking up CO_2 that is dissolved in water. Carbon may then move to the consumers that feed on the primary producers.

As plants, animals, and other organisms use the carbon in sugars for growth or movement, they respire CO_2. Furthermore, when organisms die, fungi, bacteria, and other microbes also respire CO_2 to the atmosphere as they decompose the dead organic material. The process in which organic compounds, such as sugars or dead plant and animal matter, are converted to inorganic compounds is known as *mineralization*.

Photosynthesis, respiration, and mineralization are all part of the carbon cycle (Figure 1.18). Parts of this cycle may be slow because some organic compounds in dead plants and animals can take years to decompose. Therefore, much of the carbon in ecosystems may be in the form of dead organic material, usually found in the top layers of the soil.

Topic: carbon cycle
Go to: *www.sciLINKS.org*
Code: IE06

FIGURE 1.18
The Carbon Cycle

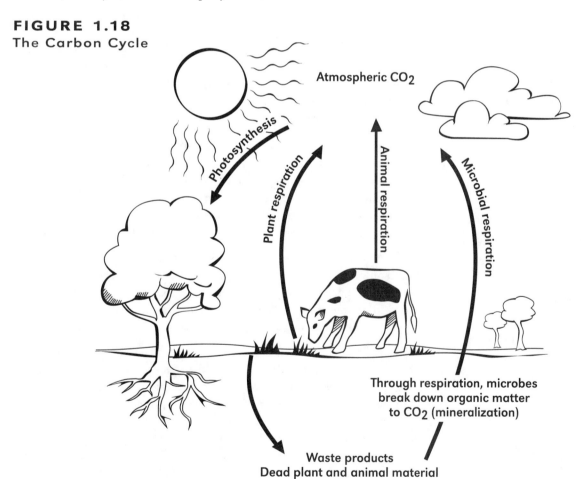

Carbon moves from the atmosphere to plants through photosynthesis and back to the atmosphere through respiration and decomposition.

THE NITROGEN CYCLE

Similar to carbon, nitrogen cycles between the atmosphere, soil, plants, and animals. *Organic nitrogen* compounds contain long chains of carbon and hydrogen, whereas *inorganic nitrogen* compounds do not. Nitrate, ammonium, and nitrogen gas are examples of inorganic compounds, and amino acids and proteins are examples of organic compounds.

Most nitrogen in the atmosphere is in the form of a gas called N_2. However, unlike CO_2, atmospheric N_2 cannot be absorbed by plants. Only a few groups of bacteria can use atmospheric nitrogen directly in a process called *nitrogen fixation*. Through nitrogen fixation, these microorganisms change N_2 to ammonia (NH_3). Interestingly, nitrogen in the atmosphere also can be "fixed" or changed to ammonia as a result of high pressures and energy generated by lightning.

Most nitrogen-fixing bacteria live in the soil, fresh water, and the ocean. However, a few of these bacteria have a special relationship with plants that benefits both the plants and the bacteria. This type of beneficial relationship is called a *symbiosis*. The microbes live in the plant's roots and supply nitrogen to the plants, while the plant supplies sugars and other carbon compounds to the microbes. (The microbes cannot photosynthesize and thus cannot produce carbon compounds on their own.) Plants that have this symbiotic relationship with microbes that fix nitrogen include alfalfa, clover, peas, peanuts, and beans, as well as alder, acacia, and locust trees. These plants are called *nitrogen-fixing* plants.

Ammonia that is fixed by bacteria or lightning is changed to ammonium (NH_4^+). Ammonium is taken up by plants and then made available to consumers. Nitrogen taken up by plants is incorporated into amino acids, which are the building blocks of proteins. When consumers eat the plants, the nitrogen, in the form of amino acids and proteins, is incorporated into their bodies.

Similar to carbon, organic nitrogen is returned to the atmosphere when plants and animals die and are decomposed. Bacteria first break the proteins and amino acids back down into ammonium. This process of changing from organic to inorganic nitrogen is called *mineralization*. (Note that the process of changing organic to inorganic carbon is also called mineralization.)

At this point, the nitrogen cycle becomes complicated because, at several different points in the cycle, the inorganic nitrogen again can be taken up by plants or further broken down. Some ammonium is absorbed directly by the plants for use in building more amino acids and proteins. What's left is further broken down by bacteria into nitrite (NO_2^-), and eventually nitrate (NO_3^-), in a process called *nitrification*. Nitrate also may be taken up by plants. Alternatively, bacteria may transform nitrate into the gaseous compounds nitrous oxide (N_2O), nitric oxide (NO), or nitrogen gas (N_2), which are released into the air. Finally, nitrate also may flow out of the soil into streams, lakes, or groundwater (Figure 1.19).

Nitrogen-fixing bacteria take nitrogen from the atmosphere and convert it to ammonia.

A symbiotic relationship between two organisms benefits both organisms.

Mineralization **is the process of converting organic carbon to inorganic carbon, or organic nitrogen to inorganic nitrogen.**

Topic: nitrogen cycle
Go to: www.sciLINKS.org
Code: IE07

FIGURE 1.19
The Nitrogen Cycle

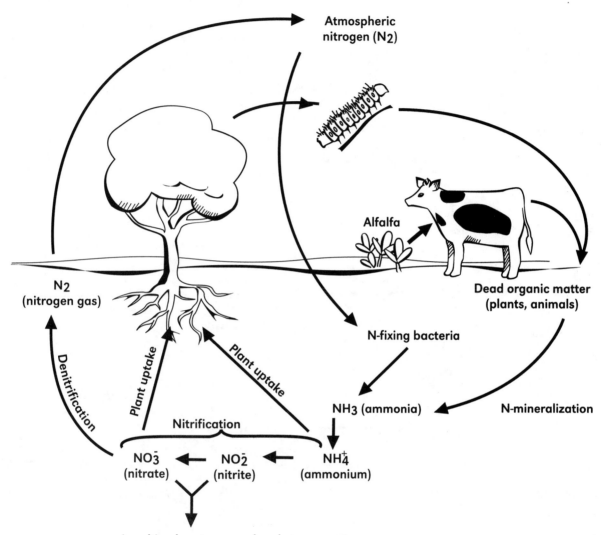

Human activities, such as agriculture or sewage disposal, can impact nitrogen cycles. Fertilizers contain ammonium and nitrate, and manure contains a lot of ammonium. In soils, ammonium is converted to nitrate. When excess fertilizer or manure is applied to soils, the nitrate may be washed into groundwater or streams and cause human health and environmental problems. Though nitrate is naturally present in most drinking water, high levels can be toxic, especially to babies. Bacteria in humans convert nitrate to nitrite, which can hinder the blood's ability to carry oxygen. Infants less than six months old are particularly affected by high levels of nitrate and may develop blue-baby syndrome (their skin develops a bluish tint) when blood oxygen levels become too low. If untreated, blue-baby syndrome can result in brain damage and even death.

Eutrophication occurs when excess nutrients cause a population explosion of algae and decomposers, which use up dissolved oxygen, causing death of fish and other organisms.

Too much nitrate also may cause environmental problems in oceans. The nitrate serves as a nutrient for algae and causes rapid algal growth. When the algae die, they are decomposed by bacteria that use up oxygen in the water. If bacterial populations get very large, they may use up so much of the available oxygen that there is little left for fish. The end result is often suffocation and massive death of fish. This process of nutrients causing rapid growth of algae populations followed by decomposition and decreased oxygen levels is called *eutrophication*. Excessive phosphorus, which, like nitrogen, is present in fertilizers, plays an important role in eutrophication of many lakes (Figure 1.20).

FIGURE 1.20
The Eutrophication Process

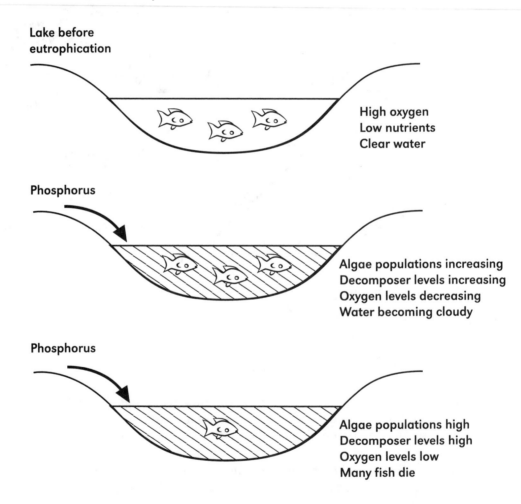

The first drawing in the figure shows a lake with low nutrient levels. In the second drawing, phosphorus begins to run into the lake (e.g., from agricultural runoff), causing populations of algae that feed on these nutrients to increase. The short-lived algae die and are decomposed by bacteria and other organisms, which use up oxygen in the lake during respiration. When decomposer levels get very high, lake oxygen levels become too low to support fish, and the fish die (third drawing).

In addition to runoff from agriculture and sewage, invasive species and biological control may impact nutrient cycles. For example, leaves of the native wetland plant cattail decay slowly after they are shed during the fall and more rapidly once temperatures warm up in the spring. In contrast, purple loosestrife leaves break down rapidly in the fall, adding a lot of nutrients to the soil at a time when there would usually be very few nutrients released. Biocontrol beetles feed on loosestrife leaves during the spring and they also add a lot of nutrients to the soil through their feces. Scientists at Cornell University are studying the results of these changes in nutrient cycling on native species and ecosystems.

EARTHWORM INVASION: CHANGING NITROGEN AND CARBON CYCLING

Earthworms provide another example of how invasive species can influence the cycling of nitrogen and other nutrients. When Europeans first settled in the northeastern U.S., they reported seeing no earthworms. This is because glaciers wiped out earthworms about 12,000 years before the Europeans arrived. Some worm species in the southern U.S. survived the last glacier age. However, because they take a long time to spread to new habitats, worms were not present in the Northeast when the Europeans settlers first made their observations.

Today, non-native earthworms are plentiful in the northeastern U.S. They have been introduced accidentally along with plants and soil brought in from Europe and other continents. The worms appear to be most common in farms and urban areas where there are many introduced plants and uncommon in isolated forests. However, earthworms currently are invading forests in the Northeast and Midwest.

Gardeners and composters love earthworms because of their role in decomposing wastes and improving soils. In fact, earthworms are extremely valuable in gardens and many soils. Yet recently, ecologists have discovered that worms may have negative impacts on forest ecosystems.

When you think of a forest, you may think of tall trees overhead. But it's also important to look down in a forest—at the *litter* layer of decomposing leaves and twigs on top of the soil. Normally, insects, worms, other invertebrates, and microbes break down the litter. When litter is broken down, nitrogen and other nutrients and energy are recycled into other parts of the ecosystem.

You have read how microbes break down organic nitrogen into ammonium and nitrate. The nitrate can be taken up by plants, changed into atmospheric nitrogen, or washed into streams, lakes, and groundwater. Many of these changes from ammonium to nitrate and N_2 gas take place in the forest litter layer.

Now enter earthworms into the forest litter. Research has shown that in soils with earthworms, more of the ammonium is converted to nitrate and eventually to nitrogen gas than in soils where no earthworms are present.

Furthermore, a microcosm experiment showed that more nitrate flows through soil to the groundwater in soils with worms. Thus, leaves and other dead organic matter are being broken down much more rapidly, and nitrate may be leaving the forests where worms have invaded. This rapid breakdown of litter can result in several problems. For example, nitrogen may leave the soil before being taken up by plants, and plants may not get enough nitrogen. Furthermore, the excess nitrate could flow into the groundwater and surface water. This can cause human health problems and eutrophication, as discussed above.

Some scientists feel that earthworms also threaten biodiversity in forests. They have observed that in forests where there used to be young tree seedlings, now there are only tall trees and bare dirt (Figure 1.21). Gone is the leaf litter where seeds are hidden from predators. The scientists have hypothesized that without the protection of the litter layer, the seeds are exposed to predators, which eat the seeds and thus prevent new plants from growing. A major difference between these sites and those in nearby areas where seedlings and small plants are still common is the presence of worms. Could it be that worms are having a major impact on new growth in our forests? How might you test this?

FIGURE 1.21
Impact of Earthworms on Forest Ecosystems

Forest without earthworms

Litter layer

Soil

Forest floor has a thick layer of decomposing and newly fallen leaves. Many small trees and seedlings are present.

Forest with earthworms

Earthworms have eaten and removed much of the leaf litter, possibly allowing seeds to be discovered and eaten by predators and preventing new plants from growing.

We can see from the earthworm story that invasive species may change carbon and nitrogen cycles. When worms change how organic material is cycled through the ecosystem, plants also may be affected. Thus, through changing soils, worms may reduce biodiversity in forests.

How can we determine the impact of earthworms on ecosystems?

Scientists in New York State are conducting a series of studies to piece together the puzzle of how worms impact forest ecosystems. Their first studies involved observations of plants and soils (e.g., whether or not litter is present) at sites with and without worms. Although they observed differences between sites with and without worms, they could not be sure that worms were the cause. What else might cause differences in forests between sites with and without worms? (Hint: Sites with worms were in urban parks and suburban areas whereas sites without worms were in forests.)

They next conducted laboratory experiments with soil from sites with and without worms. Questions they asked included: Are the levels of ammonium and nitrate different in soils with and without worms? Did soils with worms produce more CO_2 than soils without worms? (A lot of CO_2 is an indicator that decomposition is proceeding more rapidly.) Although these experiments showed differences in soils with and without worms, the scientists still could not be sure that the worms caused the differences. What if the worms just happened to be in soils with more nitrate or more rapid decomposition? Or maybe worms were attracted to such soils?

To answer these questions, the scientists conducted a controlled laboratory study. They added worms to soils and compared them to similar soils with no worms added. Results from this study provided overwhelming evidence that worms cause changes in soils. Repeating such lab experiments in the field would provide even better evidence that worms are causing changes in soil processes. What might be some of the problems and advantages of conducting such an experiment in the field?

ZEBRA MUSSELS: CHANGING WATER CLARITY AND BIODIVERSITY

Similar to earthworms, zebra mussels may impact nutrients and biodiversity. Many people have noticed that water in lakes with zebra mussels is much clearer than before the zebra mussels invaded. Why might this be so? Zebra mussels filter large volumes of water through a tube called a siphon. They take particles in with the water ranging from 10–450 microns in diameter but only digest the smaller particles (10–40 microns). The larger particles are combined with mucous and excreted back out of the siphon. These larger particles combined with mucous are heavy enough to sink to the bottom of the lake. Thus fewer particles are in the water and the water becomes clearer.

Although swimmers and boaters like the clearer water in the lake, there is also a negative side. The particles that are sinking to the bottom of the lake contain nutrients such as nitrogen. When zebra mussels cause the particles to be deposited on the bottom of the lake, the nutrients are no longer available to the plants and animals that live in the water. For example, phytoplankton are microbes that live in the water and are able to photosynthesize. They are important primary producers in lakes. Phytoplankton populations decline when there are fewer nutrients in the water. Because there are fewer primary producers, populations of consumers, such as insects and fish, may decline or even disappear from the lake. Thus, the small introduced zebra mussel may alter the entire food web in lakes, resulting in lowered biodiversity.

Zebra mussels also may directly affect biodiversity through their effects on native mussels. Zebra mussels attach to native mussels, sometimes as many as a hundred zebra mussels on one native mussel. This makes it difficult for native mussels to open and close their valves. The native mussels can no longer take in and excrete water or close their shells to protect against predators. In some lakes, this has led to near extinction of the native mussel species.

TAMARISK: CHANGING WATER DYNAMICS

Similar to carbon and nitrogen, water cycles between the living and nonliving components of an ecosystem. You are probably familiar with the *hydrologic cycle*, in which water is taken up and given off by plants and cycles through the atmosphere and soil. Some invasive species may change the hydrologic cycle and thus impact other plants and animals that depend on this cycle.

The tamarisk tree, also called salt cedar, has been in the U.S. since at least the 1850s. It originally was introduced from Europe or Asia as an ornamental plant in California. In North America, it has become invasive along streams and lakes in the dry, southwestern states.

Tamarisk outcompetes native plants, such as willow and cottonwood trees, thus reducing their populations. This has resulted in the decline of several bird species that depended on the native plants. Interestingly, several other native bird species, including one that is endangered (the southwestern willow flycatcher), now build their nests on tamarisk.

Ecosystems Analyst

Peter Vitousek studies the entire planet by carefully observing what's happening to Hawaii.

If you want to find Peter Vitousek in his lab, the first thing you have to do is go to Hawaii. After that, it gets tricky, because Vitousek's lab isn't in the state—it *is* the state. The Stanford University ecologist has devoted his career to studying the Earth's metabolism and life cycles, zeroing in on how the intricate machinery of its forests is altered by people and the introduction of new plants and animals. "Peter is a real visionary," says marine ecologist Jane Lubchenco of Oregon State University. "It's unusual to have someone who is simultaneously interested in the big picture and in taking a very detailed look at the processes themselves."

Vitousek, 52, didn't plan to spend his life tending to the planet's health; he began as a political science major. While a student at Amherst, however, he wrote a thesis on land use and stumbled across a book on biological invasions of pristine places. A native of Hawaii, he knew that this problem was especially acute in his home state. All of Hawaii's 20 species of flightless birds have vanished, and half the flying ones as well. One-sixth of the native plants are gone, and 30% of remaining ones are threatened. "I decided I wanted to be an ecologist, so I jumped into science classes to catch up," he says. "I always intended to work in Hawaii."

Now, decades later, the field is trying to catch up with him. Vitousek's studies of the Hawaiian Islands—the world's most remote archipelago and a place humans discovered only 1,500 years ago—have yielded some intriguing findings. While the arrival of new species has had the greatest impact on Hawaii's unique flora and fauna, what amazed Vitousek was how the world reaches out to touch even the most remote spots. In one celebrated study, he and his colleagues analyzed soil and rock chemistry at volcanic sites ranging from 300 years to 4.1 million years old. Plants at the youngest sites drew nutrients straight from weathering lava. Those at older, more depleted sites survived on minerals blown in on sea spray and in dust from central Asia, thousands of miles away. "No ecosystem is entirely isolated," he says.

Vitousek is currently focusing on the problem of global nitrogen, the element that makes up 80% of the atmosphere. Nitrogen is also found in fossil fuel exhaust and is a principal ingredient in fertilizer. Spread too much of it around, and it can throw off the planet's biological balance, triggering explosive growth in some species and suffocating others. "That's a huge alteration in how the world works," Vitousek says. "Our capacity to change the Earth means we must manage this." For a man who didn't even much care for science at first, that's quite a mission.

—Andrea Dorfman, 20 August 2001.

Copyright 2001 Time Inc. Reprinted with permission.

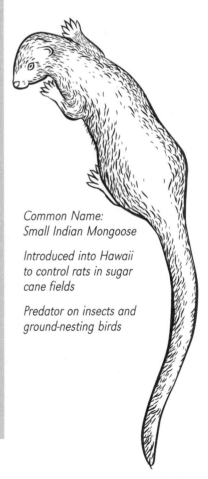

*Common Name:
Hawaiian Rail*

*U.S. Fish and Wildlife Status:
Extinct*

Last Seen: 1884

Cause of extinction probably was introduction of the mongoose in 1883

*Common Name:
Small Indian Mongoose*

Introduced into Hawaii to control rats in sugar cane fields

Predator on insects and ground-nesting birds

Tamarisk has a unique impact on streamside ecosystems in the South-west. Its roots extend into the water table where they take up large amounts of groundwater. Land managers report that springs have dried up after tama-risk invaded. Plant communities also have changed, with plants better adapted to dry conditions becoming more common after invasion by tamarisk.

Not only does tamarisk change the water dynamics, it also changes the way salt is cycled through these dry, streamside ecosystems. The tamarisk's deep roots take up salt from far down in the soil and transport it up to the leaves. When the leaves drop off the plant, they decompose on the soil sur-face and increase the salt concentration of the soil. Tamarisk plants also ex-crete salt water that falls to the ground. This increased salt concentration makes it difficult for other seeds to sprout and plants to grow. Thus, similar to the changes in water dynamics, changes in salt concentration cause changes in the plant community.

FOR DISCUSSION

▶ Refer to the invasive species profiles you developed in Chapter 3 to an-swer the questions below. While discussing the questions, record any new questions that you are not able to answer.

   a. Do any of the species you profiled have impacts on primary produc-tivity? If so, what are they? Diagram the trophic levels or carbon cycle prior to the introduction of the invasive species. Then show on the diagram how the species impacts trophic relationships and the carbon cycle.

   b. Did anyone in your group find a species that impacts nitrogen or other nutrient cycles in the ecosystems in which it is found? If so, how would you describe these impacts? Draw a diagram of the nutrient cycle and show how the species is changing it.

   c. Did anyone in your group find a species that impacts water dynam-ics? If so, draw a diagram to show how water dynamics have changed as a result of the species.

▶ As you were trying to answer the questions above, you likely were con-fronted with some new questions you couldn't answer. The answers to some of these questions may not be known. Outline a research project to answer one of these questions. Will your research include observations, experiments outdoors, and/or experiments in the lab or greenhouse?

▶ You have read about two types of impacts on aquatic ecosystems: eutrophication caused by excess phosphorus and changes in biodiversity and water clarity caused by zebra mussels. How might eutrophication be reduced? How might populations of zebra mussels be reduced? Is there a difference in our ability to control chemical pollution and "bio-logical pollution"?

CONCLUSION

Section 1 of this book included four chapters that provided information on ecology and invasive species, and some of the ways scientists conduct research to help solve problems caused by invasive species. Section 2 provides several protocols that are used by ecologists to study invasive species. Carrying out these protocols will help improve your ability to conduct research. After mastering the protocols, you can conduct a research project focusing on the biological control of invasive species, as described in Section 3. You also can use your familiarity with ecological concepts, invasive species, and the protocols to develop your own research project. Suggestions for independent research projects also are included in Section 3.

REFERENCES

Darwin, C.R. 1909–14. *The Origin of Species*. Vol. XI. The Harvard Classics. New York: P.F. Collier & Son.

Dorfman, A. 2001. Ecosystems Analyst. *Time*, 20 August.

INVASION ECOLOGY PROTOCOLS—
INTRODUCING RESEARCH

OVERVIEW

Protocols are techniques or methods scientists use in their research. It is important to understand the protocols and in many cases to practice them before embarking on an independent research project. While we have provided example research projects in Section 3, you also can design your own research projects using the protocols in this section.

Protocols 1–3 involve *fieldwork*, or work outdoors. They provide information useful in making decisions about control of invasive species. For example, the land manager at a state park needs information about what new problem species are invading the park, what invasive species already are present, how large their populations are, and the effectiveness of control measures such as herbicides or biological control.

Protocols 4 and 5 are *microcosm* experiments—they examine processes that occur in nature using soil samples in a small container. In Chapter 3, we described an example of microcosm experiments that were used to study competition between two different aquatic microorganisms. In the microcosm protocols in this book, you will measure decomposition in soil samples placed in airtight, shallow plastic containers. In microcosm experiments, you can control factors such as temperature that you are not able to control outdoors.

Safety is a concern for all field and lab work. If you are working where there are tall plants such as purple loosestrife and *Phragmites*, you should wear eye protection to avoid getting poked in the eye. Goggles and gloves should be worn for the microcosm protocols, which involve handling potentially harmful chemicals.

Protocol 1. Early Detection Surveys is a survey of an area, such as a park or nature preserve, for any problem species that might be in the process of invading. For managers wanting to control invasive species, it is important to know which species are starting to invade, because as we saw in Chapter 2, the most effective management strategy is to control small patches of invasive species before they spread.

Protocol 2. Plot Sampling—Density and Percent Cover allows you to estimate how common invasive and other species are. Plot sampling—density involves counting the stems of species within a small area (often 1 m^2) called a plot or quadrat. Plot sampling—percent cover involves estimating the percent of space in a plot that a species covers. These measures can be repeated to show changes in populations of invasive and other species over time. They also can be used to compare plant populations in different habitats or before and after different management treatments (e.g., releasing biological control insects). Before you carry out the plot survey protocol, you will learn how to locate plots using random or stratified sampling methods. By using random or stratified sampling to locate plots, you will avoid choosing plots that are close or easy to sample, which would bias your results. You also need to construct quadrat frames using PVC tubing or meter sticks prior to plot sampling.

Protocol 3. Transect Surveys involves sampling plants along a line or transect. Transect surveys can be used to determine differences in plant populations as you move from one habitat to another. For example, transect surveys could be used if you wanted to know whether the population of an invasive species changed as you moved from a disturbed roadside to an undisturbed forest. They also can be used to survey along trails, which are often the sites where invasive species are first found.

Protocol 4. Measuring Decomposition Using Soda Lime is unlike the first three protocols in that it does not involve measuring plant populations in the field. Instead, this protocol measures the rate of decomposition in a sample of organic material or soil. The amount of CO_2 produced by the sample is used to estimate the rate of decomposition. This is because the microorganisms that decompose organic matter in soil produce CO_2 and thus, the more CO_2 produced, the higher the rate of decomposition. The method used in Protocol 4 involves weighing the amount of CO_2 absorbed by a small amount of soda lime in a container with the organic material or soil sample. It requires a balance sensitive to 0.01 g. Before conducting the soda lime protocol, you will need to obtain samples of soils in the field and measure their moisture content.

Protocol 5. Measuring Decomposition Using a Titration is similar to Protocol 4 in that it measures CO_2 produced by a soil or organic material sample. However, in this protocol the CO_2 is trapped by a sodium hydroxide solution rather than by soda lime pellets. Protocol 5 uses a titration rather than a change in weight to measure the amount of CO_2 produced by the soil or organic material sample. You should be familiar with titrations before embarking on this protocol. Before conducting the titration protocol, you will need to obtain samples of soils in the field and measure their moisture content.

We suggest using shallow, airtight plastic containers to incubate soils for Protocols 4 and 5. For the titration protocol, you could use other types of airtight containers such as gallon jars, but the soda lime requires a flat container to spread out the soil. This is because soda lime is less efficient than NaOH at absorbing CO_2, and thus you need a larger soil surface area to get results.

Early detection surveys can be used to answer questions that population ecologists might ask, such as what are the abundance and distribution of an invasive species. Plot sampling and transect surveys provide more information about the abundance of species and they also can be used to answer questions in community ecology, such as how plant communities change over time. The two protocols for measuring decomposition are used to answer questions related to carbon cycles, which are important to ecosystem ecologists. Although the focus of this text is invasive species, many of the ecological questions we address also apply to other species. Thus, the plant protocols can be used to answer questions having to do with plants that aren't invasive and the soils protocols can be used to answer questions about soils that don't have invasive species. Table 2.1 summarizes the different protocols.

Before embarking on a research project, scientists generally search the library and the Internet to find out what other scientists already have learned about their research topic. You should familiarize yourself with the invasive species in your area, including what habitats they are likely to be found in, how to identify them, and what are some of the methods used to control them before conducting Protocols 1–3. (See the **Invasive Species Profile** exercise, Chapter 3, p. 40.) You might want to learn about soils in your area before conducting Protocols 4–5.

TABLE 2.1
Ecology Protocols

Questions	Protocols	Examples
What invasive species currently are coming into a local area? How widespread are they and what habitats are they invading?	Early detection surveys	Volunteers conducted a survey along the trails at a local nature center. Foresters in Chicago and New York City conducted extensive surveys of street trees to determine if the Asian longhorned beetle was present.
Are our efforts to control species x having any effect? Is the population of species x changing over time? Does the population of species x differ in different habitats?	Plot sampling— ▶ Density (useful when the number of stems is easy to count) ▶ Percent cover (useful when there are many small stems)	Scientists and students conducted plot sampling of purple loosestrife before and after releasing beetles used in biological control.
Are there any changes in what species are present as we move from one habitat to another?	Transect surveys	Garlic mustard may first invade a disturbed site along a roadside and then colonize the adjacent forest. Scientists and students could conduct a survey along a transect extending from the road into the forest.
Are invasive species changing the way carbon is cycling through the ecosystem?	Measuring decomposition	Scientists and high school students conducted a study of decomposition of soils and organic material with and without non-native worms.

INVASION ECOLOGY PROTOCOLS

PROTOCOL 1. EARLY DETECTION SURVEYS

Objective

To determine whether an invasive species is currently entering a new area.

Background

The best way to control introduced species is to destroy them when the populations are still small. But it is impossible for scientists to detect every small patch of an invasive species. Students and volunteers can help scientists by conducting early detection surveys.

An early detection survey involves *locating pest species that are in the process of invading*. Although you may want to make an estimate of the size of a population once you locate a species, early detection surveys are not designed for precisely determining population size or area covered by a species.

You should contact scientists and land managers who are likely to have lists and descriptions of invasive species in your region. These individuals may be working at universities, federal and state conservation or environmental agencies, or nonprofit groups such as The Nature Conservancy. Many states have invasive species councils that also can provide information.

Invasive species often invade areas along travel "corridors," such as roadsides, railroad tracks, or trails. This is because seeds are transported in the mud on tires or attached to animals that might use such a corridor. In addition, many invasive species are well adapted to disturbed areas, such as dirt piles next to roads or recent construction sites. Because roadsides, railroad tracks, and construction sites can be dangerous places to work, a good place to start your early detection survey is along a trail. You can contact a local park, land trust, or nature preserve to see if they have need for an early detection survey along their trails. Alternatively, after reading about the biology and ecology of a species of concern, you might be able to predict where it is likely to be found. For example, if you survey for purple loosestrife, you would want to look in wetlands and ditches, and along lakes and streams.

> CAUTION: No matter where you survey, be sure to take appropriate safety precautions. If you choose a survey along a ditch, make sure there is safe access along a trail. Stay away from active construction sites and dangerous roads.

Early detection surveys conducted along trails can be combined with plot sampling (Protocol 2) and transect surveys (Protocol 3) if you are interested in more detailed information about individual species. For example, you might determine from an early detection survey that purple loosestrife is invading along streams in your area. To then get an idea of how dense the populations are, you could conduct plot sampling.

Materials

▶ County, topographic, or other maps of area to be surveyed

▶ Copy of **Early Detection Survey Data Form 2: Summary** (p. 67)

Per student group:

▶ Section of map showing survey area (e.g., nature preserve)

▶ Multiple copies of **Early Detection Survey Data Form 1: Field Results** (p. 66)

▶ Geographic Positioning System (GPS) (optional)

Procedure

1. Familiarize yourself with the invasive species of concern in your area. In particular, focus on species that may be just starting to invade, rather than those that are already well established. It often is best to start with just one species. You should be able to find descriptions of invasive species on the Internet.

2. Contact a local environmental organization (e.g., The Nature Conservancy, land trusts), town conservation commission, state parks, state natural resources or environmental agency, state invasive species council, Cooperative Extension, or university natural resources, ecology, or environmental sciences department. These organizations likely can provide you with information on what species are of concern in your area and they may be able to help you design your survey. They might invite you to conduct a survey on their land, as your results may help them to develop management plans.

3. After gathering information from the Internet and local experts, decide which species and area should be the focus of your survey. The area could be a small watershed, nature preserve, or state park, for example. Locate the area on the county or other map.

4. Learn how to identify the species that you will be surveying. You can find photographs and descriptions of invasive species on websites. Alternatively, the organizations mentioned in Step 2 may have fact sheets on invasive species in your area. Be sure to find out what species can be seen at the time of year you sample. For example, if you sample during late fall, you may miss species such as garlic mustard that are more obvious during the spring when they flower.

5. Decide on a survey method. Because invasive species often first colonize travel corridors or sites that are disturbed, looking at these locations increases the probability you will find newly invading species. Thus, you may want to conduct trailside surveys or surveys of recently completed construction sites. You also should take into account what you have learned about the species you will be surveying through Steps 1 and 4 above. In particular, you will need to consider the habitats in which the species is found. For example, if your species only occurs in wetlands, then surveying wetlands and ditches that have safe access, and not wasting your time in forests is the best strategy. Mark the sites to be surveyed on a map of your study area.

6. Decide how to divide up the area. For example, small groups of students may have responsibility for a section of a park or a stretch of trail.

7. Walk through the sites and record information about the target species. For example, walk all the trails in the nature preserve and fill out an **Early Detection Survey Data Form 1:**

Field Results for the invasive species you are focusing on. If your species is not present along a trail or other site you have chosen, record the name and location of the site and the fact that no species of interest were found.

8. Estimate the size of the population (number of stems) and area occupied by the species (square meters) at each site you visit using the **Early Detection Survey Data Form 1: Field Results**.

9. Before moving to the next site, clean your shoes and wipe off any plant parts that may have stuck to your clothes. This is to prevent spreading invasive species to a new site.

10. Record on the map each location where your species was found. If you have access to a GPS, you can use it to help mark locations.

Data Analysis and Interpretation

Combine the data collected by the whole class. This will give you an idea of the distribution of your study species in the entire study area.

On a map of the entire area surveyed, each group should mark the sites they surveyed and the locations where the species was found. Give each location a different number. You can add different symbols next to each number, to show how large the population was (<10 stems, 10–100 stems, >100 stems) and the approximate size of the patch it occupied (<1 m^2, 1–4 m^2, 4–100 m^2, >100 m^2).

Next fill in the **Early Detection Survey Data Form 2: Summary**.

Based on the data presented on the map and in the table, is the species you surveyed coming into the study area? What sites is it colonizing? Are its populations large or small?

EARLY DETECTION SURVEY DATA FORM 1: FIELD RESULTS

Fill out this form for each species for each site you survey (e.g., trail, wetland).

Name(s) _____

Date _____

Species name _____

Study area (e.g., White Rabbit State Park, school nature preserve)

Type of site surveyed (e.g., along trail)

Brief description of site (e.g., hilly or flat, dry or wet)

Estimated number of stems of species

❏ 0   ❏ 1–10 stems   ❏ 10–100 stems   ❏ > 100 stems

Estimated size of patch

❏ 0 m²   ❏ < 1 m²   ❏ 1–4 m²   ❏ 4–100 m²   ❏ > 100 m²

Mark the location of your site on the map of the study area.

EARLY DETECTION SURVEY DATA FORM 2: SUMMARY

Class _____ Teacher _____ Date _____

Species name _____

Study area (e.g., White Rabbit State Park, Fall Creek watershed)

Type of sites surveyed (e.g., four different trails)

TABLE 2.2
Early Detection Survey

Location (number on map)	Site surveyed	Description of site (e.g., hilly, wet)	Estimated number of stems (0, 1–10, 10–100, >100)	Estimated size of patch (0, < 1 m², 1–4 m², > 4 m²)

EARLY DETECTION SURVEY: QUESTIONS

Name _____ Date _____

Species surveyed _____

_____

Answer questions 1–5 for each species you surveyed. (Please use complete sentences.)

1. Is the species you surveyed widespread or limited to just a few locations?

2. Describe areas or habitats where the species is likely to be found (e.g., near opening in forest).

3. Are populations of the species relatively large or small?

4. Do you notice any patterns in the abundance and distribution of species? What factors, or processes, may account for these patterns? (E.g., resources such as water and light, seed dispersal, reproductive rates.)

5. Does your map show sites that you surveyed and where you did not find the species, in addition to sites where you did find the species? If you only showed sites where you found the species, what information might be lost in trying to interpret your results?

6. Can you suggest a management strategy for this species? Use the results of the survey, what you know about the species, and what you know about large and small patches (see p. 20) to answer this question.

7. What additional information might you need to better plan a control strategy? How might you get this information?

EARLY DETECTION SURVEY: QUESTIONS *(continued)*

8. If you found sites where your species was not present, were there any differences between those sites and the sites where the species was present?

9. If you were going to repeat this survey, what would you do differently? How might you improve the methods to get more reliable results?

10. Cite or document the references you used to find information about the species you surveyed. Which references do you think are most reliable? Why?

PROTOCOL 2. PLOT SAMPLING— DENSITY AND PERCENT COVER

Sampling

Sometimes it is too time-consuming, expensive, or even impossible to collect data from your entire study area. Sampling allows us to gain information about a site without looking at every plant or animal. Sampling involves taking measurements on small plots that are representative of the larger study area and using the data to represent the entire study area. By locating quadrats using random or stratified sampling, you increase your chances of getting a representative sample. What might be the problem if you chose sampling locations without first setting up a sampling scheme (e.g., by choosing the first spot you encountered or by choosing sites that had lots of the plants you were interested in)?

Objective

To estimate population size or relative importance of invasive and other species in a study area.

Background

How do scientists measure the size of plant populations? Scientists could count every individual plant, but imagine how long this would take in large areas with many plants. When conducting plant ecology research, scientists often select smaller sample plots inside the larger study area. The scientists thoroughly study the plants in the sample plots and then use these results to make generalizations about the entire area.

For plants that are large, relatively easy to count, and not too numerous (less than 100 individuals per m^2), scientists count each stem in the plot to determine density (number of plants per area). When the plants are small and numerous (e.g., clovers, grass, or moss), it is extremely difficult to count each individual stem. In these cases, scientists estimate the percent of the ground covered by the species. In any one plot, you can measure density for plants with stems that are easy to count and percent cover for plants that are too hard to count. However, you must use the same method for the same species for all plots and you can't compare species measured using different methods.

In this protocol, we have included instructions for measuring density and percent cover in 1 m^2 plots. If plants are extremely dense so that it is difficult to count stems or estimate percent cover, you can decrease the size of the plots. For example, you may want to use 0.5 m^2 (0.5 m x 1.0 m) or 0.25 m^2 (0.5 m x 0.5 m) plots. If the plants are sparse and you are not getting a good sample, you can increase the size of the plots.

Prior to breaking into student groups to estimate density and percent cover, you should practice making these estimates as a larger class. There are several tricks that you can use to make these measurements easier. For example, you can start at one end of a plot and use a stick to separate stems you have already counted from those you haven't yet counted. To estimate percent cover, you can practice using a square quadrat frame with 10 cm intervals marked off (see below). Percent cover can be difficult to estimate at first, and getting practice beforehand will make things go more smoothly in the field.

When you practice the protocols with other students, you will likely come up with several different questions about exactly how to sample the plants. Making decisions about these details as a class will help standardize how different student groups collect data. This will allow you to combine data from different plots to get averages for the entire study area. It also will make it possible to compare results from different sites.

Prior to making measurements on plants, you will need to locate your study plots. There are many ways to locate small sample plots in a larger study area. Using an accepted method to locate these small plots can help to avoid bias. For example, imagine a research project on the side of a steep mountain. Getting to plots at the top of the mountain takes more effort than getting to plots closer to the bottom, so at the end of a long day of fieldwork, researchers might—perhaps unknowingly—select more plots near the bottom. To avoid this and other types of bias, scientists have developed several methods to locate plots in a larger study area.

Random sampling is one way to locate plots. To randomly select plots, scientists first determine how many plots they want, and then use random numbers to locate them. For example, scientists may first walk a random number of steps along the edge of their study area. Then they choose another random number and walk that many steps into the study area. The sample plot is located at the final step (see Figure 2.1).

FIGURE 2.1.
Random and Stratified Sampling

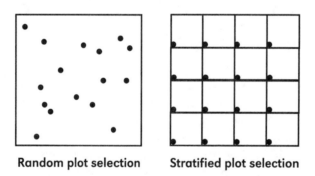

Random plot selection   Stratified plot selection

Each of the study areas has 16 plots represented by the black dots.

The biggest drawback to random plot selection is the possibility that, by chance, all the plots will be clumped or located near each other. Selecting plots using *stratified sampling* is a way of avoiding clumping. When using stratified sampling, scientists randomly locate a starting point and then divide their study area into a certain number of equal boxes. They next locate a plot at the corner of each box.

After locating your sampling plots, you will need to build quadrat frames. Then you will count stems and estimate percent cover of different species on your sampling plots.

PART 1. LOCATING SAMPLE PLOTS—RANDOM AND STRATIFIED SAMPLING

Random Sampling

Materials

▶ Stakes and flagging

▶ Random number table *or* stopwatch *or* phone book

Procedure

1. Locate the corner of the study area in which you will sample (e.g., a wetland).

2. Orient yourself so that you will walk along the longest edge of your study area.

3. Choose a random number using one of the methods described below. If the edge of your study area is less than 99 paces, you will need a random number between 00 and 99. If the number you choose is larger than the maximum number of steps you can take along the edge of your study area, choose the next random number. For example, if your study area is 60 paces long and you choose random number 71, select the next number.

   a. **Random number table.** Locate a random number table, often located in ecology or biology laboratory textbooks. Pick any number on the page, and for each subsequent number you need, choose the next number below.

   b. **Stopwatch.** Using this method you only will be able to generate random numbers with two digits. Obtain a digital stopwatch that measures to the nearest one hundredth of a second. Press the start button, wait a while, and press the stop button. Your two-digit random number is determined by using the digits in the tenth and hundredth places.

   c. **Phone book.** If you do not have access to a random number table or a stopwatch, you can use the white pages (not the pages that contain advertisements) of a phone book. Flip the book open, and choose a name at random. Your random number is determined by choosing the last digits of the phone number. For each subsequent random number you need, choose the next number below.

4. Beginning at your starting point and continuing along the edge of your study area, walk the number of steps indicated by your random number.

5. Turn 90 degrees towards the plot. Choose another random number (use the next number in the table or phone book, or use the stopwatch method again), and walk the number of steps indicated by this second number. You should be walking into your study area in a direction that is perpendicular to the edge of the plot. Walk in a straight line. Try not to veer to the right or left to avoid shrubs or wet spots.

6. The corner of your first sampling plot is located where your foot lands on the last step. You may want to permanently mark the corners of your plot with stakes and flagging. Avoid trampling plants in the plots. Repeat steps 3–6 to locate additional plots.

Making Decisions

Whenever someone measures plants in the field, questions are bound to come up about how to conduct the measurements. Should I stretch out the plant when I am measuring its height or just measure it as is? What do we mean by "stem" when the plant branches part way up? Should I measure percent cover at ground level or as seen from above the plants?

The answers to these questions will vary, depending on why you are measuring something. Ask yourself why you are taking a certain measurement. Are you measuring percent cover to get an idea of the amount of bare soil surface that might be available for a seed to sprout? Or is percent cover important as a measure of how shaded smaller plants might be. Depending on your objectives, would you want to measure percent cover at ground level or higher up?

For some questions there may not be one good answer. However, regardless of the question, the class will need to come to a consensus so that all measurements are collected in the same way. The class should write down all these questions and the decisions that were made, so that next year's students will be able to continue the study in the same way. This will allow you to make comparisons from one year to another.

Making decisions like this is part of conducting research.

Stratified Sampling

Materials

▶ Stakes and flagging

▶ Map of site

▶ Surveyor's tape (100 m or 50 m) or nonstretch string

Procedure

1. Obtain or make a map of your study site and determine the outside dimensions.

2. Decide how many sample plots you will need. Later on, you will divide the study area into a grid of equal-sized squares. You will locate one sample plot in each square.

3. Choose a random number and walk that many steps to start the grid. Next divide your study area into a grid of equal-sized squares, one for each sample plot. You may want to first draw out the grid on a map of the site. Then using a survey tape, nonstretch string, or pacing off the correct distances, mark the edges of the squares with stakes and flagging. Avoid trampling and disturbing the study area as much as possible.

4. Locate a sample plot at the corner of each of the sections of your study area.

Observer Bias

If several different groups of students estimate density or percent cover of the same species on the same plot, do they get different results? You might want to try this in your class and see how close the results are for density and percent cover. Whenever someone measures plants in the field, there is bound to be some error due to differences in the way different researchers take their measurements. When several people are working on the same research project, they often train together so that their measurements are more standardized.

PART 2. BUILDING QUADRAT FRAMES

Materials (per student group)

▶ ½ in PVC tubing, elbows, and sleeves *OR*

▶ Meter sticks, or other sticks 1 m in length and screws or nonstretch string

Procedure

1. A quadrat frame will mark the outer edges of your plot. You can build a square quadrat frame out of PVC tubing or meter sticks. One method involves fastening sections of PVC tubing using elbows. To make the quadrat frame easier to slide under vegetation, you can construct the two halves separately using PVC tubing and sleeves. Both halves are in the shape of a square "C." Using right-angle elbows, attach both ends of a 1 m piece of tubing to 0.5 m long pieces of tubing. Place sleeves at the end of the 0.5 m pieces so they can be joined in the field to form a square. Another method used to construct quadrats is tying 1 m long pieces of string between both ends of two meter sticks (Figure 2.2). This method is best for short vegetation as the strings may get caught on taller plants. Another method is to fasten meter sticks to each other using screws.

2. Regardless of the method used to construct the quadrats, make sure they can be taken apart or folded up for carrying. It is best to leave one corner of the quadrat unattached so you can unfold the quadrat and slide it under the vegetation into place. If all four sides are fixed, you must place the quadrat over the vegetation, which can be difficult with tall plants such as purple loosestrife.

3. Mark 10 cm intervals on your quadrat frame in black and the 50 cm point in red to help you estimate percent cover. For example, by marking off every 10 cm, you can visualize a square 10 cm x 10 cm, which is the same as 1% cover for a 1 m² plot. A rectangle that is 50 cm x 10 cm is 5% cover, a square 50 cm x 50 cm is 25% cover, and so on.

FIGURE 2.2
Quadrat Construction

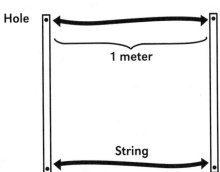

Hole

1 meter

String

Cut string into two 130 cm lengths. Firmly tie string to the holes in the ends of the meter sticks. Be sure your final string length is 1 m. Leave one string end untied so you can place the quadrat around tall vegetation.

PART 3. PLOT SAMPLING

Materials (per student group)

▶ Quadrat frame

▶ Copies of **Plot Sampling Data Form 1: Density and Percent Cover** (one for each plot) (p. 78)

▶ Copy of **Plot Sampling Data Form 2: Summary** (p. 79)

Procedure

1. Decide how many plots (also called quadrats) you will sample. A rule of thumb is either a minimum of ten plots or one 1 m^2 plot per 100 m^2. Divide into groups of 3–4 students for 1 m^2 plots. Each student group should be responsible for one or more plots. Students in each group should take on roles as data gatherers and data recorders.

2. Locate the sampling plot using either the random or stratified selection methods described above.

3. Lay out the 1 m^2 quadrat on the ground at the first sampling point you have chosen. Be careful not to step in the quadrat while laying it out.

4. For species that are easy to count and that are tall, count the number of stems in the plot. Record this number separately for each species on the **Plot Sampling Data Form 1: Density and Percent Cover.** If the stems are numerous, you can avoid double counting by starting at one corner of the plot and moving systematically across the plot. You also can hold or mark stems you have counted, or place a plastic wand or thin stick between the counted and uncounted stems.

5. If the species is very numerous and not too tall, estimate what percent of the area of the plot it is covering (its percent cover), rather than count individual stems. Record the percent cover separately for each species on the **Plot Sampling Data Form 1: Density and Percent Cover.** For any one species, be sure to use the same method (density or percent cover) on all plots so you can make comparisons. You can use percent cover for smaller species and density for larger species in the same plot but you will not be able to compare species that are measured using different methods.

6. Repeat steps 2–5 for each plot you are responsible for sampling.

7. If you encounter species you cannot identify, (a) describe the species (e.g., 1 m tall, purple flowers), (b) collect a sample from outside your plots, (c) try to identify the species using identification keys or by asking experts, and (d) press the specimen for use as reference for future surveys.

DATA ANALYSIS AND INTERPRETATION

You can use the data from your plot surveys to make generalizations about density and percent cover in the larger study area. To do this, you will need to compile the results for all the plots in a particular area. You can determine the average density or percent cover for each of the species you measured for all your plots.

After gathering together all the plot sampling data forms, calculate the average density or percent cover for each species found in your large study area using the formula below.

(You may substitute percent cover for density where appropriate but don't mix cover and density.)

Average species density $= \dfrac{\text{(density in plot 1) + (density in plot 2) + (density in plot X)}}{\text{total number of plots}}$

For example, consider a series of 5 plot surveys conducted in a schoolyard. Purple loosestrife was found in 4 of the plots.

Plot #	Species	Density (#/m²)
1	Loosestrife	85 stems/m²
2	Loosestrife	53 stems/m²
3	Loosestrife	64 stems/m²
4	Loosestrife	33 stems/m²
5	Loosestrife	0 stems/m²

Average species density $= \dfrac{85 + 53 + 64 + 33 + 0}{5} =$ **47 stems / m²**

On the **Plot Sampling Data Form 2: Summary**, record the average density or percent cover for each of the species you found in your study area. You can use the average density to compare different species, to compare the same species from several different sites, and/ or to compare sites where control measures have and have not been implemented. You can use average percent cover in the same ways. However, you cannot compare species measured using density with species measured using percent cover.

PLOT SAMPLING DATA FORM 1: DENSITY AND PERCENT COVER

Complete one form for each plot.

Name(s) _____ Date_____

Description of study area (e.g., wetland) _____

_____

_____

Plot ID number/label _____

Description of sample plot (e.g., standing water, shady) _____

_____

_____

Method used (density, percent cover, or both) _____

_____

Species name (or description)*	Density (# of individuals in plot)	Percent cover (% of plot covered by species)

If you don't know the name of the species, you can describe it and give it a name. You may want to take a sample of the species to later determine its name by asking an expert or using a field guide.

PLOT SAMPLING DATA FORM 2: SUMMARY

Use one form to compile the results from all individual plot surveys for each study area (e.g., schoolyard or wetland).

Class _____ Teacher _____ Date _____

Description of study area (e.g., wetland) _____

_____

_____

Number of plots surveyed _____

Determine the average density *or* percent cover for each species using the formula in **Data Analysis and Interpretation** (p. 77).

Species name (or description)	Average density	Average percent cover

PLOT SAMPLING DATA FORM 2: SUMMARY *(continued)*

Draw a bar graph showing the average density or percent cover of the different species.

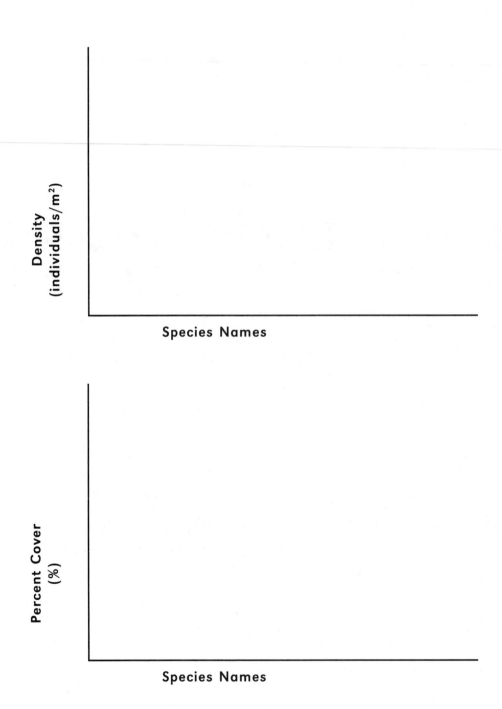

PLOT SAMPLING: QUESTIONS

Name _____ Date _____

(Please use complete sentences.)

1. Did you find any species that were present in all plots or had very high densities? Give some reasons that might explain this.

2. Did you find any species that were not present in all plots or had very low densities? Give some reasons that might explain this.

3. How did the density (or percent cover) of the invasive species compare with the other species in the study area?

PLOT SAMPLING: QUESTIONS *(continued)*

4. Do you think the combined results of all your plot surveys accurately represent the larger study area? Please explain. What might be some problems with the data you collected?

5. If you were to do your sampling again, what things might you change? Why might you make these changes?

6. Do you think plot sampling is a good way to study large areas? Why or why not? Explain.

PROTOCOL 3. TRANSECT SURVEYS

Objective

To estimate the relative abundance of species in your study area.

Background

Transect surveys consist of walking along a straight line and recording the plants you encounter along the line. They can be used to determine changes in plant species related to changes in habitats. For example, you might hypothesize that the number of invasive species will decrease along a line or transect that goes from a disturbed roadside into an undisturbed forest. Transect surveys can be conducted in three different ways. You can record

1. Whether a species is present at specific points (e.g., every 0.5 m along the transect)

2. Whether a species is present within a specific interval (e.g., within each 0.5–1.0 m segment along the transect)

3. The number of times and length along the transect that a species occurs (e.g., species occurs from 0.5–0.6 m from start of transect and again from 0.8–1.0 m from start of transect).

The first method is the easiest but gives the least information, whereas the last method requires the most work and provides the most information.

Below we present instructions for conducting a transect survey where you record whether the species is present at specific points along a transect. We assume that you are working in a more or less rectangular study area and that different student groups will conduct replicate transect surveys within the study area. You could alter the instructions to conduct a transect survey along a trail. For example, you might work with a park ranger to set up a transect survey to determine where along a trail you find the invasive species garlic mustard. You could record which 100 m segments of the trail had garlic mustard within 2 m of the trail. You could even combine a transect survey along a trail with a second transect survey at right angles from the trail to determine if garlic mustard populations decrease with distance from the trail.

For any transect survey, you can use a tape measure (e.g., 50 m or 100 m) or nonstretching string. Alternatively, you can determine the length of your pace and use the number of steps you walk to estimate distances along a transect. To determine your pace, first make a mark on the ground. Starting with your heel at the mark, walk 20 steps in a straight line. Mark the point where the tip of your toe lands on the 20th step. Measure the distance from the start to the end of your 20 steps. Divide this number by 20 to determine your pace. Repeat this several times to get an average. Then use your average pace to estimate distances along a transect. For example, if one step is 50 cm, 200 steps would be about 100 m. If you are sampling off a trail, try to avoid excess trampling of vegetation. Avoid sites where there are rare or fragile species if a lot of students will be trampling off a trail.

At several points in the protocol, we present options for sampling in slightly different ways. When you are conducting the transect survey in the field, you may come up with questions that are not addressed in the protocol. For example, does a plant have to touch the transect line, or will you sample individual plants within 0.5 m of the transect? You can choose from the suggestions we present or devise other ways to sample, but all groups should use the same sampling methods if you want to compare your results. Thus, a discussion of exactly what methods you will use prior to sampling is essential.

Materials

▶ Copy of **Transect Survey Data Form 2: Summary** (for multiple species and transects) (p. 89)

Per student group:

▶ Tape measure or nonstretch string with marks showing every 0.5 meters

▶ Compass (optional)

▶ Meter sticks

▶ Copies of **Transect Survey Data Form 1: Field Results** (p. 87)

Procedure

1. Depending on the question you are trying to answer, decide what species you will be recording and how the transects should be located. For example, if you want to determine changes in an invasive species as you move from a disturbed to an undisturbed site, locate the transect so that it crosses from the disturbed into the undisturbed site and has roughly the same length in both sites (Figure 2.3). It is much easier to conduct a survey for just one species, so starting with a single species is a good idea. Later on, you may want to add additional species to your transect survey. You may want to conduct multiple transects parallel to each other to get a more representative measure of the distribution of the species in your sampling area.

FIGURE 2.3
Example Transect Arrangement

2. Construct a map of your sampling area. Record the length, orientation, and location of the transects on the map. Divide into groups of 2–4 students and have each group take one or more transects.

3. Lay down a tape measure or marked string along the transect line. You can use a compass to lay out the line. Try to avoid trampling individual plants before they are accurately recorded. One way to do this is to walk on the left side of the tape and only record plants on the right side of the tape. Alternatively, you could walk 0.5 m away from the tape and record the plants that are up to 0.5 m on either side of the tape.

FIGURE 2.4
Example Transect Running through Two Patches of an Invasive Species

Sample area

Transect line
(Tape measure or marked string)

0   0.5   1.0   1.5   2.0

Distance along transect (m)

Invasive species patch

This is an example transect running through two patches of an invasive species. The species should be recorded as "present" at 1.0 m, and "absent" at all other transect points.

4. Record the presence or absence of the invasive or other species of interest every 0.5 m along the transect (i.e., at 0.0 m, 0.5 m, 1.0 m, etc.). You will need to decide what determines whether a species is "present" before beginning this protocol. For example, you may consider plants to be present if they are within 0.1 m of the transect point or you may mandate that a plant is present only if its stem, branches, or leaves are located exactly above the transect point (Figure 2.4).

5. If the vegetation in your site is not very dense, you may want to walk along the line carrying a meter stick perpendicular to the line. You can then record the presence or absence of the invasive species within 0.5 m on either side of the transect intervals (Figure 2.5).

FIGURE 2.5
Recording Presence of Invasive Species

Sample area

0   5   10   15   20   } 1 meter

Meter stick

Patches of the invasive species that fall within 0.5 m to either side of the transect are recorded.

6. Each time you record the presence of a plant, also record the type of habitat (e.g., closed forest, open forest, roadside, wetland). All the groups should determine a consistent way to record the different types of habitats in your sample area before beginning the protocol.

7. When you have completed the transect survey, draw on your map where the species of interest was located. Show where the different habitats are on the map also.

Data Analysis and Interpretation

You can use your data to determine how common the species was along the transects using **Transect Survey Data Form 1: Field Results**. You also can detect changes in the species you measured as you move from one habitat to another. Looking at your results and maps showing the location of species and habitats along the transects, can you make any generalizations about where your species is likely to occur? Were the results from the different transects similar or was there a lot of variability?

If you sampled two or more species, you can use your data to give an indication of what species are most common along the transect. For each transect, count up the total number of points at which any one species occurred (A). Then calculate all the possible points in the particular transect (B). Next calculate the proportion of points at which you found the invasive species by dividing A by B (A/B). Finally, determine the average proportion of points where the species occurred for all transects combined. Record this information on the **Transect Survey Data Form 2: Summary**.

TRANSECT SURVEY DATA FORM 1: FIELD RESULTS

Complete one form for each species along each transect.

Name(s) _____ Date _____

Species name _____

Name of study area _____

Transect number _____

Transect length _____

Total number of sampling points along your transect _____

Describe your study area (e.g., disturbed roadside to undisturbed wetland)_____

_____

_____

Describe how you recorded the presence of species along the transect (e.g., presence or absence within 1 m to each side of transect, every 0.5 m along transect)

_____

_____

_____

List points where species was present	List points where species was absent (e.g., 0.5 m, 2.0 m)	Habitat

TRANSECT SURVEY DATA FORM 1: FIELD RESULTS *(continued)*

Total number of points species present along transect, A = _____

Total number of points along transect, B = _____

Percent points where species was present
(points species present/ total points along transect), A/B _____

Habitats where species was commonly found _____

_____

_____

_____

_____

_____

Habitats where species was rarely found _____

_____

_____

_____

_____

_____

Habitats where species was not found _____

_____

_____

_____

_____

_____

TRANSECT SURVEY DATA FORM 2: SUMMARY

For more than one species and transect

Use one form to compile the results from all individual transect surveys for each study area.

Class _____ Teacher _____ Date _____

Name of study area _____

Total number of transects _____

Total length of all transects combined _____

Total number of sampling points along all transects _____

Describe your study area (e.g., disturbed roadside to undisturbed wetland)_____

_____

_____

Describe how you recorded the presence of species along the transect (e.g., presence or absence within 1 m to each side of transect, every 0.5 m along transect)

_____

_____

Species name	Average % of points where species found along all transects	Habitats where species commonly found	Habitats where species occasionally found	Habitats where species not found

TRANSECT SURVEY: QUESTIONS

Name _____ Date _____

(Please use complete sentences.)

1. For the species you sampled in your transect survey, give an overall description of where it was located along your transects.

2. If your transects included both disturbed and undisturbed habitat (e.g., went from a road into an adjacent forest), describe how your species varied with respect to disturbance. Was it present in the greatest numbers near the disturbed site or away from the disturbed site? Give some reasons that could explain these results.

3. If you were to conduct transect surveys again, would you do anything differently? Why? There are several different suggestions in the background to this protocol (pp. 51–72) for how you could conduct the transect surveys. How do you think the method you chose would compare with the other options?

4. Under what conditions do you think transect surveys are a useful tool for measuring the presence of invasive species? How might they compare to other methods for surveying invasive species (e.g., early detection surveys, plot surveys)?

PROTOCOL 4. MEASURING DECOMPOSITION USING SODA LIME[1]

Objective

To determine decomposition rates in soil and organic material.

Background

Soil consists of both inorganic material and organic material. The inorganic material comes from rocks that have been broken down to smaller particles. The organic material comes from living things in the soil. For example, plants shed leaves and drop twigs onto the soil. When they first drop onto the soil, the twigs and leaves are called litter or the litter layer. Eventually, they decompose and become part of the organic material in the soil. When plant roots die, they also become part of the organic material in the soil. Additional organic material is added when invertebrates that live in the soil, such as worms and ground beetles, die. Finally, many different organisms add organic matter to the soil in the form of feces and other waste products.

When microbes and invertebrates break down organic matter in soil, they produce CO_2 through the process of respiration. Thus, the rate at which CO_2 is produced in soil is a good indicator of the rate of decomposition of organic matter in the soil.

We present two methods for measuring CO_2 in soils: soda lime (Protocol 4c) and titration (Protocol 5). In the soda lime protocol, the CO_2 is "trapped" or absorbed by soda lime, and you determine how much CO_2 was produced by measuring the weight gain of the soda lime. Because the weight gain is small, the soda lime protocol requires a metric balance that measures to 0.01g. In the titration protocol, CO_2 is again trapped, this time by sodium hydroxide solution. You then conduct a titration to determine how much CO_2 was trapped. To do the titration, you will need a basic understanding of chemistry and some experience performing titrations.

In both protocols, you will measure the CO_2 produced by microbes and invertebrates in a *microcosm*—in this case, an airtight plastic container. A microcosm is a small-scale laboratory model of what occurs in nature.

Both protocols involve three steps:

▶ Obtaining soil and worm samples (Protocol 4a)

▶ Determining soil moisture content (Protocol 4b)

▶ Measuring CO_2 production (Protocol 4c or 5)

---

[1] This protocol was adapted from Tibilske, L.M. 1994. Carbon mineralization. In *Methods of Soil Analysis*. Part 2. Ed. R.W. Weaver, 841-844. Madison, Wis.: Science Society of America, Inc.

Why use a microcosm experiment?

Ecosystems can be difficult to study because they are often large and have many factors (e.g., moisture, temperature) that are changing at the same time. Thus, it is difficult to conduct a controlled experiment where you vary only the one factor in which you are interested.

Because ecosystems are so difficult to study, scientists create "mini-ecosystems" or *microcosms*. A microcosm is a small-scale model of a larger ecosystem. For example, an aquarium, plastic container, or gallon jar with soil can be used to conduct microcosm experiments. When conducting experiments in microcosms, it is possible to vary only the one factor you are interested in and to keep other factors constant.

It is important to keep temperature, moisture, and other conditions in the microcosm as close as possible to field conditions. This will help ensure that results from microcosm experiments resemble what actually happens in nature. Microcosms are most appropriate for studying the effects of physical and chemical factors on small organisms and interactions among small organisms.

PROTOCOL 4A. OBTAINING SOIL AND WORMS

Introduction

This protocol describes how to take soil samples to be used in the soda lime and titration CO_2 protocols. It also describes how you can sample worms in the field or purchase them for experiments comparing CO_2 production in soils with and without worms.

Materials (per student group)

◗ Soil or bulb corer, or knife and lid of wide-mouthed mason jar

◗ Rubber spatula or trowel

◗ Plastic wrap

◗ Plastic containers with lids for storing soil samples

◗ Plastic containers with lid and holes for collecting worms

◗ Ziploc or other sealable bags

Procedure

1. Before taking soil samples, decide the purpose of your sampling. For example, do you plan to compare soils from various locations or from various depths at a single site? Soils vary with depth, so the depth of sampling is an important consideration. On top of the soil, you will find a flattened layer of partially decomposed leaves. Right below this organic layer, the soil is likely to be deep brown or black because of its high organic matter content. This is where you would expect the rates of decomposition to be the highest. Further down below the surface, soils are likely to be gray or light brown because they contain much less organic matter and therefore support less life. (Soil changes with depth will vary depending on the type of soil and where you are in North America.)

2. To take a sample of partially decomposed leaves, first brush away the undecomposed, intact leaves or "litter." To take a sample of soil, scrape away the litter layer and partially decomposed leaves.

3. To take the sample, lay the lid of a wide-mouthed mason jar or similar round object on the soil. Use a knife or a small (keyhole) saw to cut out a "cookie" of organic soil around the lid, cutting as deep in the soil as you need. Then carefully use a trowel, your fingers, or a rubber spatula to lift the sample out. Alternatively, you can use a soil corer available through a garden supply store.

4. Wrap each sample in plastic wrap and label it. Place in a plastic container. It is important to keep soil as intact as possible because microbial activity in the soil is dependent on soil structure.

5. Proceed with Determining Soil Moisture Content (Protocol 4b) and then with Measuring CO_2 Using Soda Lime (4c) or Titration (Protocol 5, p. 106).

6. If you want to test the effect of worms on decomposition, you will need to locate a source of worms. The best time to look for worms is in spring or during a wet summer. In some areas, you may have forest soils with and without worms. Forest soils without worms generally have an intact layer of the current or previous year's leaves over a more decomposed organic layer. Forest soils with worms generally look disturbed on the surface and the organic layer may be missing or mixed with the mineral layer. Worms also leave "castings" (waste products) on the soil surface. Castings look like small piles or pellets of soil. After seeing these telltale signs of earthworms, dig through the soil to see if you find any worms.

7. Collect extra soil for the worms to live in while in the lab. Gather worms and place them in Ziploc plastic bags for returning to the lab. You may notice there are several species of worms and decide to separate worms by species.

8. Once back in the lab, place worms in a plastic container with air holes until you are ready to perform your experiments. Provide them with soil to burrow into.

9. If no worms are present, you may want to purchase worms. You can try different kinds of worms, for example, night crawlers sold for bait and red worms (*Eisenia foetida*) sold for composting.

NOTE: After the experiment DO NOT discard purchased worms in the forest. You do not want to introduce worms to areas where they are not already present. Use them for bait or put them in a compost pile away from the forest.

PROTOCOL 4B. DETERMINING SOIL MOISTURE CONTENT

Introduction

If you are measuring decomposition in soils, why do you need to measure soil moisture content? One reason is because it allows you to calculate the dry weight of your sample, a number that is used in the formula for determining the rate of CO_2 production.

Another reason for measuring moisture content is that moisture greatly affects the rate of activity of soil microbes. Slightly moist conditions provide the best environment for most soil microbes. If soil becomes too dry, the microbes become dormant. When conditions are too wet, lack of air creates an environment in which only microbes that don't need oxygen can survive. By calculating the moisture content of a subsample of soil, you can determine if you have to add water to your larger sample, if you should allow it to dry out, or if it already has the right conditions for microbial growth and decomposition.

Materials

▶ Metric balance with 0.1 or 0.01 g accuracy

▶ Drying oven or microwave

▶ 10–20 g soil sample

▶ Beakers

▶ Spoon or scoop for handling soil

▶ Distilled or unchlorinated water (if needed for Part 2)

▶ **Measuring Decomposition Using Soda Lime Data Form 1: Soil Moisture Content** (p. 100)

Procedure

Part 1. Determine percent moisture using a subsample

In this procedure you will use a subsample of your soil so that you will still have some left to measure CO_2 production. All weights should be measured to the nearest 0.1 g.

Mix your soil thoroughly and remove any large chunks such as pebbles or roots. Fill in the top section of the **Measuring Decomposition Using Soda Lime Data Form 1: Soil Moisture Content** and then use the form to record the measurements and calculations you make in the following steps.

1. Label and record the weight of a small beaker.

2. Weigh 10–20 g of your soil directly into the beaker. Record the exact weight of the beaker and soil. Subtract out the weight of the beaker to determine the weight of the soil. (This is the *wet weight*.)

   Wet wt of soil subsample = combined wt of beaker and soil – wt of beaker

3. Dry the soil using either a drying oven or microwave. If using a drying oven, dry the sample for 24 hours at ~100°C. If using a microwave oven, drying time will vary. First heat the sample on *low power* for 5 minutes, allow to cool, and then weigh it. (It is essential to use low power so that the soils do not reach a high enough temperature to burn or release anything other than water.) Then keep heating for one additional minute and weigh the sample at each interval. Repeat this cycle until the weight change before and after heating is minimal.

4. After drying, record the weight of the beaker and the soil. Subtract out the weight of the beaker to determine the weight of the soil. (This is the *dry weight*.)

Dry wt of soil subsample = combined wt of beaker and soil after drying – wt of beaker

5. Calculate the moisture content using the following equation:

$$\text{Moisture content} = \frac{\text{wet wt} - \text{dry wt}}{\text{wet wt}}$$

This result is expressed in decimal form for use in dry weight and CO_2 calculations. To express as a percentage instead, simply multiply by 100.

6. If the soil contains more than 90% water, it is too wet. Spread your larger sample out in a thin layer and allow it to dry at room temperature out of direct sunlight until it looks moist but not wet. Repeat steps 2–6 with a new subsample after the soil has dried, to determine if the desired % moisture has been reached. If the soil is still too wet, continue the drying process until the moisture content is near 50%.

7. If the soil contains less than 10% moisture, follow Part 2 below to figure out how much water to add.

8. If the soil is in the 10–90% moisture range, proceed to Protocol 4c or Protocol 5 to measure the CO_2 production rate.

Part 2. Adjust total sample to 50% moisture
(Perform only if soil moisture content is <10%; see step 8 above.)

In Part 2, your calculations and adjustments will be for your full sample (not the subsample used in Part 1 above).

1. Weigh your total soil sample. This is the *total soil weight*.

2. Calculate the actual water weight in your total sample using the moisture content you determined in Part 1.

Actual water wt of full sample = total soil wt of full sample x moisture content of subsample

3. Find the total *dry* weight of your soil sample.

Dry wt of full sample = total wt of full sample – actual water wt of full sample

4. For a 50% moisture sample, the desired water weight is equal to the dry weight of the sample. If your % moisture is too low, determine how much water you need to add by using this calculation:

Wt of water to be added = desired water wt – actual water wt

5. Add the amount of water needed. If possible, use distilled or bottled water, especially if your tap water contains chlorine. To weigh water, first weigh a beaker and then slowly add water until you have the correct weight (beaker + water – beaker).

6. Gently sprinkle the calculated amount of water into the entire soil sample, and mix thoroughly.

7. Let the soil sit for 24 hours to allow microorganisms to regain activity before beginning Protocol 4c or Protocol 5 to measure the rate of CO_2 production.

PROTOCOL 4C. MEASURING CO_2 USING SODA LIME

Introduction

CO_2 is produced in soil by microbes and other organisms as they break down organic material. Therefore, the rate at which CO_2 is produced provides an indication of the rate of decomposition in soil. In this protocol, soda lime reacts with CO_2 being respired by the organisms in the soil. The change in the weight of the soda lime over the 48-hour incubation period can be used to estimate the amount of CO_2 respired by the soil microbes and other organisms.

Soda lime is made up of sodium hydroxide (NaOH) and calcium hydroxide ($Ca(OH)_2$). When exposed to air, it undergoes the following reactions:

$$2NaOH + CO_2 \rightarrow Na_2CO_3 + H_2O$$

$$Ca(OH)_2 + CO_2 \rightarrow CaCO_3 + H_2O$$

As the above equations indicate, when soda lime reacts with CO_2, it gains weight both from the formation of Na_2CO_3 and $CaCO_3$ and through absorbing the water that is produced. However, soda lime also absorbs moisture from the air, which has nothing to do with the reactions with CO_2. To correct for the weight gain from atmospheric water, the soda lime must be dried at the end of the protocol. Because this evaporates both the water absorbed from the air and the water produced during the CO_2 reaction, the weight of the dry soda lime underestimates the total weight gain caused by CO_2. To correct for this, you will need to multiply the dry soda lime weight gain by a correction factor of 1.69.

To account for atmospheric CO_2, you will create a blank by placing soda lime in an airtight container with no soil sample. Then you will follow exactly the same procedures as those used for the soil samples. The "blank" soda lime will tell you how much CO_2 is in the air when the containers were first sealed. You will subtract this from the results you get from the containers containing soil samples.

Materials

▶ Metric balance accurate to 0.01 g

▶ Soil sample (enough to cover airtight container to a depth of 1 cm)

For each soil sample:

▶ 1 shallow, wide, *airtight,* plastic container (approximately 25 cm x 25 cm)

▶ 1 glass petri dish or watch glass (microwave-proof)

▶ 20 g soda lime

▶ Spoon or scoop for handling soil

▶ Drying oven or microwave

▶ Gloves

▶ Goggles

▶ **Measuring Decomposition Using Soda Lime Data Form 2: Blanks** (one per blank) (p. 102)

▶ **Measuring Decomposition Using Soda Lime Data Form 3: Samples** (pp. 103–104)

▶ **Measuring Decomposition Using Soda Lime Data Form 4: Summary** (one for all samples in a single treatment) (p. 105)

Procedure

There are four parts in this procedure: creating blanks, preparing the soda lime, preparing the soil samples, and incubating the samples with the soda lime. Note that you need to have the soil samples and soda lime ready to be put together in the airtight container at the same time. Therefore, after preparing the soil samples, prepare the soda lime immediately. The changes in soda lime weight will be very small (in the order of tenths of a gram). Therefore, it is essential that you follow the instructions exactly, being careful to obtain and record accurate weights, and to time the steps as specified.

Part 1. Create Blanks

For every five soil samples you should create one blank. Follow the directions below except do not use any soil and do not record the weight of the airtight container. Simply place a dried dish of soda lime into an empty airtight container like the ones you are using for soil samples, then label and seal it. Place this empty container with the others and after 48 hours, follow steps 2-4 in the Incubate Soils with Soda Lime section below. The *blank soda lime weight gain* that you calculate will account for the background level of CO_2 in the air.

Part 2. Prepare Soil Samples

1. Just before measuring the dry weight of the soda lime, mix the soil thoroughly.

2. Record the weight of the airtight container (without lid) to the nearest 0.1 g.

3. Spread the soil sample in the airtight container to approximately 1 cm thickness. Record the weight of the soil and container to the nearest 0.1 g. For each sample, fill out the top section of a **Measuring Decomposition Using Soda Lime Data Form 3: Samples**.

Part 3. Prepare Soda Lime

> **Note:** Before beginning this section of the protocol, put on gloves and protective eyewear.

1. Record the weight of a petri dish bottom to the nearest 0.01 g.

2. Add about 20 g of soda lime to the petri dish and leave uncovered. If you will be measuring CO_2 respiration for several soil samples, try to use the same amount of soda lime for each (within 0.5 g). Record the weight of the soda lime and petri dish to the nearest 0.01 g.

3. Dry the petri dish with the soda lime in a microwave or drying oven. If using a drying oven, the sample should be dried for 24 hours at ~100° C. If using a microwave, heat the sample for 2 minutes on LOW power. Weigh it. Heat for an additional minute. Weigh the sample again. Repeat this cycle until the change in weight before and after heating is minimal.

4. Immediately after drying the soda lime, record the dry weight of the soda lime and petri dish bottom to the nearest 0.01 g. Since soda lime absorbs water from the air, it should be used immediately after completing this step.

Part 4. Incubate Soils with Soda Lime

1. Place the uncovered petri dish and soda lime gently on the soil in one corner of the container. Place the lid on the container and make an airtight seal, being careful not to spill any soda lime out of the petri dish. Allow it to sit for 48 hours at room temperature out of direct sunlight.

2. After 48 hours, remove the dish containing soda lime from the airtight container. Brush off any soil that is stuck to the outside of the petri dish, then dry the soda lime again, either in a drying oven for 24 hours at ~100°C or in a microwave (see step 3 under Prepare Soda Lime above).

Part 5. Calculate the Amount of CO_2 Produced

(These calculations can be carried out on the data forms.)

1. Immediately after drying, measure the combined weight of the dried soda lime and petri dish to the nearest 0.01 g.

2. Subtract the weight of the dried soda lime before the 48-hour incubation period from the weight of the dried soda lime after the incubation period. This will be a very small number and is known as *sample soda lime weight gain*.

$$\text{Sample soda lime wt gain} = \text{wt of dried soda lime after incubation with soil} - \text{wt of dried soda lime before incubation}$$

3. The soda lime weight gain of the blank is referred to below as the *blank soda lime weight gain*. If your soda lime blank decreased or did not gain any weight, this means your ambient CO_2 levels were very small, and your blank soda lime weight gain is zero. If you used more than one blank, calculate the average blank soda lime weight gain and use it below.

$$\text{Blank soda lime wt gain} = \text{wt of dried soda lime after incubation with soil} - \text{wt of dried soda lime before incubation}$$

4. For samples, calculate the *corrected soda lime weight gain* using the following formula:

$$\text{Corrected soda lime wt gain} = \text{sample soda lime wt gain} - \text{blank soda lime wt gain}$$

5. Calculate the total dry weight of the soil you used.

$$\text{Dry wt} = \text{total soil wt} - (\text{ moisture content} \times \text{total soil wt})$$

For example, if the moisture content of a soil sample weighing 20 grams is 60%, then

$$\text{Dry wt} = 20 \text{ g} - (0.60 \times 20 \text{ g}) = 8 \text{ g}$$

6. The amount of CO_2 produced can be calculated using the following formula:

$$CO_2 \text{ respiration} = \frac{(\text{milligrams } CO_2) \times 1.69 / (\text{\# of days})}{(\text{kilograms dry soil})}$$

(Multiplying by 1.69 corrects for evaporation of the water produced during the reaction of soda lime and CO_2. See introduction to this protocol for an explanation.)

If you plan to repeat this protocol, you can keep reusing the same soda lime until it has increased by ~7% of its original mass. After this occurs, new soda lime should be used.

Data Analysis and Interpretation

Calculate the average CO_2 produced. If you measured CO_2 production for several different treatments (such as soil with and without worms), you should calculate the average for each treatment separately. You can also make a graph showing each value you obtained and the average, to get an idea of variability among samples.

MEASURING DECOMPOSITION USING SODA LIME DATA FORM 1: SOIL MOISTURE CONTENT

Complete one form for each soil sample.

Name(s) _____

Date _____

Soil sample ID number _____

Soil sampling location _____

Type of area sampled (e.g., forest, schoolyard) _____

Date soil sample was collected _____

Description of soil sample (e.g., number and size of rocks and roots in sample; was the soil very wet or very dry?)

_____

_____

Was the soil sample well mixed?_____

Date and time soil subsample placed in drying oven _____

Date and time soil subsample removed from drying oven _____

OR time and power level required to dry subsample in microwave

_____

Protocol 4b, Part 1. Determine percent moisture, using a subsample

Step 1.*
Weight of beaker   =   _____ g

Step 2.*

Wet wt of soil	=	combined wt of beaker and soil	−	wt of beaker
	=	_____ g	−	_____ g
	=	_____ g		

Step 4.*

Dry wt of soil subsample	=	combined wt of beaker and soil after drying	−	wt of beaker
	=	_____ g	−	_____ g
	=	_____ g		

---

* Step numbers refer to those in the Part 1 procedure, starting on p. 95.

Step 5.

$$\text{Moisture content} = \frac{\text{wet wt - dry wt}}{\text{wet wt}} = \frac{\_\_\_\_ \text{ g} - \_\_\_\_ \text{ g}}{\_\_\_\_ \text{ g}}$$

Moisture content = _____

This figure is highlighted because it will be used in calculations on other data forms. It is expressed in decimal form for use in other calculations.

Protocol 4b, Part 2. Adjust total sample to 50% moisture, if needed

Step 1.*

Total soil wt = _____ g

Step 2.*

Actual water wt of full sample	= total soil wt of full sample	x moisture content of subsample
	= _____ g	x _____
	= _____ g	

Step 3.*

Dry wt of full sample	= total soil wt of full sample	– actual water wt of full sample
	= _____ g	– _____ g
	= _____ g	

Step 4.*

Wt of water to be added	= desired water wt	– actual water wt
	= _____ g	– _____ g
	= _____ g	

* Step numbers refer to those in the Part 1 procedure, starting on p. 95 and the Part 2 procedure on p. 96.

MEASURING DECOMPOSITION USING SODA LIME
DATA FORM 2: BLANKS

Complete this form for each blank.

Name(s) _____

Date _____

Protocol 4c, Part 3. Prepare soda lime

Before incubation

Weight of petri dish bottom   = _____ g

Weight of dish and soda lime before drying   = _____ g

Weight of dish and soda lime after drying **(A)**   = _____ g

Protocol 4c, Part 5. Calculate the amount of CO_2 produced

After incubation and redrying of the soda lime

Weight of dish and soda lime   = _____ g

Weight of dish and soda lime after redrying **(B)**   = _____ g

Blank soda lime wt gain (C)   = **B – A** = _____ g

MEASURING DECOMPOSITION USING SODA LIME
DATA FORM 3: SAMPLES

Complete this form for each soil sample.

Name(s) _____

Today's date _____

Soil sampling ID number _____ Sampling date _____

Soil sampling location _____

Type of area sampled (e.g., forest, schoolyard) _____

Soil description _____

Date and time soda lime incubation started _____

Date and time soda lime incubation ended _____

Total # days incubation (should be 2 days) _____

Protocol 4c, Part 2. Prepare soil samples

Before incubation

Weight of container (without lid) (**G**)   = _____ g

Weight of container (without lid) and soil (**H**)   = _____ g

Total soil wt (I)   = H − G = _____ g

Protocol 4c, Part 3. Prepare soda lime

Before incubation

Weight of petri dish bottom   = _____ g

Weight of dish and soda lime before drying   = _____ g

Weight of dish and soda lime after drying (**J**)   = _____ g

Protocol 4c, Part 5. Calculate the amount of CO_2 produced

After incubation and redrying of the soda lime

Weight of dish and soda lime   = _____ g

Weight of dish and soda lime after redrying (**K**)   = _____ g

Sample soda lime wt gain (L)   =   K − J = _____ g

MEASURING DECOMPOSITION USING SODA LIME
DATA FORM 3: SAMPLES *(continued)*

Calculating the rate of CO_2 production

1. Calculate the corrected weight gain for soda lime using:

Corrected soda lime wt gain	=	sample soda lime wt gain	–	blank soda lime wt gain
Y	**=**	**L**	**–**	**C**
_____ g	=	_____ g	–	_____ g

The answer will be in grams of CO_2 produced. For use in the final equation, you'll need to convert this to milligrams:

_____ g x 1000 mg/g = _____ mg CO_2

2. Calculate the dry weight of the total soil sample (using soil weights from this form and moisture content from Part 1, step 5 on the **Measuring Decomposition Using Soda Lime Data Form 1. Soil Moisture Content**):

Dry wt = total soil wt – (moisture content x total soil wt)

$Z = I - (moisture\ content \times I)$

____ g = ____ g – (____ x ____ g)

This answer will be in grams of dry soil. For use in the final equation, you'll need to convert it to kilograms:

_____ g x 0.001 kg/g = _____ kg dry soil

3. Calculate the rate of CO_2 production in milligrams CO_2 produced per day per kilogram of dry soil. Use your answers from the previous two steps in place of the Y and Z in this equation:

$$CO_2\ production\ rate = \frac{Y\ mg\ CO_2 \times 1.69/days\ incubated}{Z\ kg\ dry\ soil} = _____\ mg\ CO_2/day/kg\ dry\ soil$$

MEASURING DECOMPOSITION USING SODA LIME
DATA FORM 4: SUMMARY

Use this form to compile results from all of your soil samples. If your sample ID #s represent replicates of the same soil, then you can average the CO_2 production rates. If your experiment involved using treatments, such as measurement of decomposition rates in soil containing worms vs. without worms, then you should take averages of any replicates within each treatment.

Name(s) _____ Date _____

Class _____ Teacher _____

Date soil samples were collected _____

Describe the soil samples listed on this page. Include soil sampling location, a description of the location, and any other useful information (such as sampling depth or observations about soil conditions at the sampling site).

Describe soil type or treatments

Soil sample ID#	Treatment	Corrected soda lime wt gain (mg CO_2)	Days incubated	Total soil sample dry wt (kg)	CO_2 production rate (mg CO_2/ day/kg dry soil)

PROTOCOL 5. MEASURING DECOMPOSITION USING A TITRATION[1]

Objective

To determine decomposition rates in soil and organic material.

Background

This protocol uses sodium hydroxide (NaOH) to trap CO_2 and a titration to determine decomposition rates in soil. Because microorganisms and small invertebrates respire CO_2 as they break down organic material, rates of CO_2 production are a good indicator of decomposition rates. (For a more complete explanation, we suggest you read Measuring Decomposition Using Soda Lime, Background, p. 92, prior to conducting this protocol.)

Before carrying out this protocol, you will first need to obtain a soil sample (Protocol 4a) and determine its moisture content (Protocol 4b). You will then measure the CO_2 produced by microbes and invertebrates in a microcosm—in this case, an airtight plastic container. A microcosm is a small-scale laboratory model of what occurs in nature. You will leave the NaOH with the soil in the microcosm for a 24–48 hour "incubation period."

> **NOTE:** You should practice titrating before carrying out this protocol. The acid (HCl) and base (NaOH) used in this titration are at low concentrations (1 M), but you should still wear safety goggles, gloves, and laboratory aprons, and should work in a well-ventilated area. As with any lab activity involving acids, you should have easy access to a spill kit.

In this protocol, you will use the reaction of CO_2 with NaOH to measure the amount of CO_2 released from the soil. CO_2 produced by the microbes and invertebrates in soil reacts with NaOH as shown in the following equation:

$$2\,NaOH + CO_2 \rightarrow 2H^+ + CO_3^{2-} + 2\,Na^+ + O^{2-}$$

You will begin this protocol with a known quantity of NaOH in a beaker in your soil microcosm. Because CO_2 reacts with NaOH to form carbonic acid (H_2CO_3), the solution becomes less basic as it absorbs CO_2. Next, you will add strontium chloride ($SrCl_2$) to the solution. $SrCl_2$ reacts with CO_3^{2-} to form an insoluble precipitate. This removes all CO_3^{2-} from solution and prevents the equation equilibrium from moving back to the left.

Next you will add phenolphthalein to the solution. Phenolphthalein is pink in basic solutions and clear in solutions that are neutral. When you first add phenolphthalein to your solution, the presence of NaOH will cause the solution to turn pink. Then you will titrate (or add know quantities of) HCl into the solution. When the solution develops a neutral pH, it will turn clear. By measuring how much acid you need to add before the solution becomes neutral, you can find out how much CO_2 was absorbed during the incubation period.

You will use blanks to account for background levels of CO_2 in an empty container.

---

[1] This protocol was adapted from Trautmann, N., and M. Krasny. 1998. *Composting in the Classroom.* Dubuque, Iowa: Kendall/Hunt Publishing Company; and Paul, E. A. et al. 1999. The determination of microbial biomass. In G. P. Robertson et al. (eds). *Standard Soil Methods for Long-Term Ecological Research.* New York: Oxford University Press.

Materials

For the incubation

▶ Metric balance accurate to 0.1 g

▶ Soil samples (~100 g for each titration)

▶ Thermometer

▶ Gloves

▶ Goggles

▶ Incubator (optional)

For each soil sample:

▶ 1 shallow, wide, *airtight,* plastic container (approximately 25 cm x 25 cm)

▶ Beaker to hold NaOH (needs to fit inside the airtight container with air space above)

▶ 20 mL 1M NaOH

▶ 10 or 20 mL pipette

> **NOTE:** For every 5 soil samples, you will need to create a "blank." Each blank requires an additional airtight container and beaker with NaOH .

For titrations

▶ Magnetic stirring plate and bar (optional)

▶ Gloves

▶ Goggles

▶ **Measuring Decomposition Using Titration Data Form 2: Summary** (p. 112)

For each soil sample:

▶ 20 mL 1M HCl

▶ 2 mL 1M $SrCl_2$

▶ Phenolphthalein

▶ 20–50 mL buret or "Poor Man's Buret" (Flinn Catalog #AP8752)

▶ **Measuring Decomposition Using Titration Data Form 1: Samples** (pp. 110–111)

Procedure

There are three components to this protocol—preparing blanks, preparing soil samples, and titrating. You should prepare your blanks and soil samples at the same time. After incubating them for 24–48 hours, you should run titrations on all samples and blanks at the same time. The exact amount of incubation time can vary but it is essential that you incubate all the samples you will be comparing for the same amount of time.

Part 1. Preparing Blanks

For every five soil samples you should create one blank. For each blank you will follow the directions for "preparing soil samples" below except that you will not use any soil. Simply place a beaker of NaOH in an airtight container and seal it. Leave this empty airtight container with the others, and follow steps 3–7 from the **Preparing Soil Samples** procedure and steps 1–7 from the **Titration** procedure below.

Part 2. Preparing Soil Samples

1. Weigh the bottom of the airtight container to the nearest 0.1 g.

2. Mix soil sample thoroughly, and then transfer ~25 g into the airtight container. Record the total weight of the bottom of the container and soil sample combined, to the nearest 0.1 grams.

3. Using a pipette, transfer 20 mL of 1M NaOH solution into a beaker.

4. Place the beaker containing NaOH into the airtight container with soil. The container must be tall enough to allow airspace above the NaOH beaker when the container is sealed. Be careful not to spill any NaOH.

5. Tightly seal the airtight container. Record the date, time, and temperature. Be sure to create one blank (with NaOH but no soil) for every five soil samples.

6. Store airtight containers with soil and NaOH at room temperature (20–30ºC) or warmer if possible. You want to provide a constant warm temperature. A sunny windowsill is not appropriate because it will get hot during the day and cold at night. An incubator set at 37ºC is ideal. One possibility is to create your own incubator using a light or heating pad in a box.

7. After the soil samples have incubated for 24–48 hours, you will measure the amount of CO_2 absorbed by each NaOH trap. This is accomplished by titrating with 1M HCl according to the procedure outlined below.

Part 3. Titration

When you are ready to titrate, open the airtight container, remove the beaker containing NaOH, and proceed with the instructions below. Also follow this procedure for your blanks. Do not open the airtight container until you are ready to titrate that sample's NaOH and try to titrate all samples as closely together in time as possible. The accuracy of your results depends largely on how careful you are with the titrations.

1. Record the date and time the incubation ended.

2. Add 2 mL of 1M $SrCl_2$ to the NaOH solution. A white precipitate should form.

3. Add 2–3 drops of phenolphthalein indicator to the NaOH solution. The phenolphthalein should cause the solution to turn pink.

4. Fill the buret with 1M HCl and zero it. Titrate very slowly with the acid until the NaOH solution begins to become clear. Frequently swirl or use the magnetic stirrer to mix the solution while adding acid.

5. As the endpoint gets closer, add HCl one drop at a time, mixing thoroughly between drops. The endpoint has been reached when the solution turns from pink to clear. The

greater the amount of CO_2 that has been released from the soil and has reacted with the solution, the less acid it will take to reach the titration endpoint.

6. Record the molarity of HCl used (should be 1M) and the volume of HCl required to reach the endpoint (clear solution).

7. Calculate your results using the **Measuring Decomposition Using Titration Data Form 1: Samples**.

Data Analysis and Interpretation

Calculate the average CO_2 produced. If you measured CO_2 production for several different treatments (such as soil with and without worms), you should calculate the average for each treatment separately.

MEASURING DECOMPOSITION USING TITRATION
DATA FORM 1: SAMPLES

Complete this form for each soil sample.

Name(s) _____ Date _____

Soil sample ID number _____

Soil sampling location _____

Type of area sampled (e.g., forest, schoolyard) _____

_____

Date soil sample was collected _____

Protocol 5, Part 2. Preparing Soil Samples

1. *Calculate dry weight of soil.*

Weight of container without lid (**G**) = _____ g

Weight of container without lid
and soil (**H**) = _____ g

Total soil weight (H-G) = _____ g

Use total soil weight and % soil moisture from Part 1, step 6 on the **Measuring Decomposition Using Soda Lime Data Form 1: Soil Moisture Content** to calculate dry weight of soil. Remember to use the fraction for moisture content (not multiplied by 100).

Dry wt (g) = total soil wt – (moisture content x total soil wt)

= _____ g

This answer will be in grams of dry soil. For use in the final equation, you'll need to convert it to kilograms:

Dry wt (kg) = dry wt (g) x 0.001 kg/g

= _____ kg dry soil

Protocol 5, Part 3. Titration

2. *Record the amount of time you used for the incubation.*

   Date and time incubation began _____

   Date and time incubation ended (should be 24–48 hours)_____

   Length of incubation period = _____ **days**

   (# of days incubated. e.g., 27 hours = 1.125 days)

3. *Calculate the CO_2 produced by soil samples and present in the blank(s).*

   Molarity of HCl used in titration _____

   (This should be 1. If different, ask your teacher for help in altering the final CO_2 respiration equation.)

   Milliliters HCl used to titrate blank (**B**) _____

   (If you used more than one blank, determine the average and record it here.)

   Milliliters HCl used to titrate sample (**S**) _____

   CO_2 produced in milligrams = (B-S) x 22*

   $\qquad\qquad\qquad\qquad$ = (_____ mL - _____ mL) x 22

   $\qquad\qquad\qquad\qquad$ = _____ mg

4. *Calculate the CO_2 production rate.*

   The CO_2 production rate is the rate of CO_2 produced in milligrams CO_2 per day per kilogram of dry soil. Use the kg dry soil from step 1, number of days incubation from step 2, and mg CO_2 from step 3 above.

   $$CO_2 \text{ production rate} = \frac{[(CO_2 \text{ produced in milligrams})/(\# \text{ of days incubated})]}{(\text{kilograms dry soil})}$$

   $$= \underline{\qquad} (\text{mg } CO_2 / \text{ day}) /\text{kg dry soil}$$

*You may wonder why there is a "22" in the equation. It is necessary to convert from milliliters HCl into milligrams CO_2 as shown in the following equation:

$$(\text{HCl}_{blank} - \text{HCl}_{sample}) \times 22 = (\text{HCl}_{blank} - \text{HCl}_{sample}) \times \frac{1 \text{ liter}}{1000 \text{ mL}} \times \frac{1 \text{ mol HCl}}{\text{liter}}$$

$$\times \frac{44 \text{ g } CO_2}{\text{mol } CO_2} \times \frac{1 \text{ mol } CO_2}{2 \text{ mol HCl}} \times \frac{1000 \text{ mg}}{\text{g}}$$

MEASURING DECOMPOSITION USING TITRATION DATA FORM 2: SUMMARY

Use this form to compile results from all of your soil samples. If your sample ID #s represent replicates of the same soil, then you can average the CO_2 production rates. If your experiment involved using treatments, such as measurement of decomposition rates in soil containing worms versus without worms, then you should take averages of any replicates within each treatment.

Name(s) _____   Date _____

Class _____   Teacher _____

Describe the soil samples listed on this page. Include soil sampling location, a description of the location, and any other useful information (such as sampling depth, or observations about soil conditions at the sampling site).

_____

_____

_____

Date soil samples were collected _____

Soil type or treatment _____

Sample ID	Treatment	CO_2 produced (mg)	Days incubated	Total soil sample dry wt (kg)	CO_2 production rate (mg CO_2/ day/kg dry soil)

MEASURING CO$_2$ PRODUCTION (SODA LIME OR TITRATION): QUESTIONS

Use this form for Protocol 4 and Protocol 5.

Name _____ Date _____

(Please use complete sentences.)

1. Describe the general results of the soda lime or titration experiments. What did you learn about soil CO$_2$ production rates?

2. Were CO$_2$ production levels higher or lower than you expected? Explain.

3. If you had replicates for each treatment or soil type, what was the average for each treatment or soil type? What does the average tell you about differences between treatments or soil types?

MEASURING CO$_2$ PRODUCTION (SODA LIME OR TITRATION): QUESTIONS *(continued)*

4. Did you see any variability among soil samples in the same treatment or soil type? Give some reasons to explain this variability.

5. If you measured CO$_2$ in different treatments (e.g., presence or absence of worms, litter versus soil), explain your results. Which treatment had higher levels of CO$_2$ production? What are some possible reasons for the differences?

6. If you were to do either of these protocols again, what would you do differently? Would you use different treatments? Make some predictions for how production levels could vary between treatments.

7. Why is the measurement of soil decomposition rates useful or important? Explain.

PROTOCOL PLANNING AND PEER REVIEW FORMS

Ask your teacher where each of these forms fits in the Environmental Inquiry research process.

Forms for the individual protocols can be found at the end of each protocol.

PROTOCOL PLANNING FORM

Name _____ Date _____

1. What is the name of the protocol you will be using?

2. What is the purpose of this protocol?

3. What question are you hoping to answer using this protocol?

4. You will be using your protocol to

   ❑ Survey existing conditions

   ❑ Compare conditions in two or more different habitats or ecosystems

   ❑ Perform an experiment in the laboratory

   ❑ Perform an experiment in the field

PROTOCOL PLANNING FORM (*continued*)

5. Describe the species you will be studying. (If there is more than one species, give the following information for each species in the space provided below.)

   Name of species:

   Problems it may cause:

   Habitats in which it is found:

6. Describe the field sites or lab setup you will be using.

DATA ANALYSIS PEER REVIEW FORM

Name _____ Date _____

Are the data presented clearly?

Very clear	❏	Comments about what was done well:
Mostly clear	❏	
Somewhat clear	❏	Suggestions for improvement:
Largely unclear	❏	

Are the conclusions clearly stated?

Very clear	❏	Comments about what was done well:
Mostly clear	❏	
Somewhat clear	❏	Suggestions for improvement:
Largely unclear	❏	

Do the data clearly support the conclusions?

Very clear	❏	Comments about what was done well:
Mostly clear	❏	
Somewhat clear	❏	Suggestions for improvement:
Largely unclear	❏	

BEYOND PROTOCOLS—
CONDUCTING INTERACTIVE RESEARCH

IDEAS FOR INVASION ECOLOGY RESEARCH

Many types of ecological research are possible using the early detection surveys, plot sampling, transect surveys, and decomposition protocols. In this chapter, we first provide some ideas for interactive research and pointers for developing your research project. We suggest that you start by filling out the **Choosing a Research Topic** form (p. 160) and then read the sections below that cover topics of interest to you.

We also have presented complete instructions for two research projects focusing on the biological control of invasive species. These projects were chosen because they are ongoing projects being conducted by Cornell scientists in cooperation with high school and middle school students.

EARLY DETECTION SURVEYS AND LONG-TERM MONITORING

As a result of global travel and trade, new species are constantly being introduced into North America. Some of these become established and invade new areas. Thus, the species newly invading your area will change over time, as will the populations of species that become established. You may want to set up a long-term monitoring program for your school or community. You can use the early detection survey combined with plot sampling and transect surveys and develop a system for storing your data in hard copy and electronic files. You may want to set up a website about your project, including the methods for collecting data, the actual raw data, and data summaries and reports. Students in future years can use the system you set up to track annual changes in newly invading species and populations of established species.

This project may be best conducted in partnership with a conservation organization, such as a land trust or The Nature Conservancy, with a state park, or with a government agency such as a department of conservation. These organizations and agencies may be able to use your data in planning management actions and to assist you in identifying species and areas to focus your efforts on. Another possibility is to use an area of your schoolyard that is not landscaped to follow changes in invasive species over time.

PLOT SAMPLING AND TRANSECT SURVEYS

Plot sampling allows you to focus on ecological processes in a single habitat, such as a wetland or schoolyard. With plot sampling, you can simply follow changes in an area that occur over time without any intervention by humans or major natural disturbance. Alternatively you can compare two habitats that differ in some way. When comparing two different habitats, you are, in effect, conducting an "experiment" similar to experiments you might conduct in the laboratory, but with some important differences.

In laboratory experiments, scientists look at the effect of one factor at a time. For example, in an experiment to test the effect of light on growth of plants, scientists vary only the light levels for the different plants. They keep other factors, such as temperature and fertilizer, constant for all the plants.

Laboratory experiments also use *treatments* and *controls*. For example, if you are measuring the effect of fertilizer on plant growth, you would want to add fertilizer to some plants; these plants are called the treatment plants. You would leave other plants untreated as the control plants. This allows you to compare the growth of plants that have been fertilized to the growth that would have occurred anyway with no fertilizer

Finally, when conducting experiments in the laboratory, scientists use *replicates* of each treatment and the control. They take the average result from all the replicates for the treatment and compare it to the average from all the replicates for the control. By having replicates, scientists avoid reaching false conclusions on the basis of one case.

When conducting research in the field, scientists try to vary only one factor and to include controls and replicates. However, it is not as easy to follow these guidelines for experiments in the field as it is for experiments in the lab. This is because there is a lot of variability we cannot control when conducting experiments outdoors. Experiments in the field also may take lots of time and scientists may have to settle for fewer replicates than would be ideal. Despite these drawbacks, field experiments provide valuable insights into processes that occur in nature.

Following are some ideas for field "experiments" that could be conducted using plot sampling protocols.

Changes in species composition following efforts to reduce populations of invasive species

Government agencies or conservation organizations (e.g., land trusts) may be attempting to reduce populations of invasive species at sites in your community by burning, applying herbicides, or using biological control. Your class might embark on a community service project in cooperation with land managers to help control an invasive species. (Note: Here we are using the word "control," not as a control in an experiment, but as a means for reducing populations of a species.) By setting up permanent plots on the site, you can help the land managers determine the results of their control strategies.

If possible, it is good to sample plant density and percent cover prior to implementing the control measure—these "before" measurements serve as a *reference* (similar to an experimental control) that you use to compare with the results of the actions taken to control the invasive species. Alternatively you can compare sites where attempts have been made to control invasive species to reference sites that have been left alone.

Comparison of species composition in sites where deer are excluded by a fence and in sites left alone

Some Cooperative Extension offices, university field stations, and nature preserves set up fenced areas to keep out deer. These "exclosures" are used as demonstration sites to show the effect of deer browse on the growth and regeneration of trees and other plants. Students can conduct surveys to compare plant species and plant growth inside and outside the deer "exclosures."

Comparison of species composition along a transect from field to forest, or from disturbed to undisturbed site

Species composition may change dramatically as one moves from an open site, such as a field, to a closed site, such as a forest. Similarly, species may change as one moves from a disturbed to an undisturbed site. Early successional, often invasive species that prefer open areas may extend a short way into the forest due to higher light levels at the edge of a forest. Sometimes species that were originally present in disturbed sites may eventually invade less disturbed sites. You can conduct a transect study to determine whether invasive species are limited to disturbed sites, such as along roadsides, or have invaded forests and less disturbed sites.

DECOMPOSITION STUDIES

Decomposition studies using microcosms are conducted indoors in the lab. It is easier to vary only one factor at a time and to include controls and replicates in the lab than in field studies. However, like other laboratory experiments, decomposition experiments may not represent exactly what happens under natural conditions in the field. (Why might an experiment conducted in a lab not predict exactly what would happen in nature?) Thus, scientists sometimes combine laboratory experiments with field experiments to better understand how processes occur in nature. Below are issues you might address using decomposition studies.

Comparison of decomposition rates in soil with and without earthworms

Earthworms may have a dramatic effect on decomposition in forest and garden soils and in compost. You can choose soil, leaves, or compost samples and add worms to one half of the samples to determine the effect of worms. You should try to control factors other than worms that might affect your results, such as whether or not you took samples from similar layers in the soil, the weight of the worms, soil moisture, and temperature. You can compare the effect of different species of worms on decomposition rates.

Comparison of decomposition rates in litter and mineral soil, wetland and forest soils, and at varying temperatures and moisture contents

Decomposition rates will vary depending on the amount and type of organic material, temperature, and moisture content in soils. You could test the effect of these and other factors, such as light levels, inoculating mineral soil with different organic materials, and soil texture (e.g., sand and clay), on decomposition.

PURPLE LOOSESTRIFE PROJECTS

BIOLOGICAL CONTROL OF PURPLE LOOSESTRIFE—BACKGROUND

You can join the efforts of scientists and volunteers across North America who are researching the effect of biocontrol beetles on purple loosestrife. Contact the Cornell Biological Control of Nonindigenous Plant Species program, *www.invasiveplants.net*, for information on current research and ways to contribute to the Cornell effort. There also may be local groups that you can collaborate with that are conducting purple loosestrife control efforts, such as your state natural resources agency. The research steps include

1. Collecting baseline data on the plants at the site where you will release the insects

2. Growing purple loosestrife plants in "cages" made of mosquito netting

3. Raising leaf-feeding insects on the purple loosestrife in the "cages"

4. Harvesting the new insects and releasing them onto purple loosestrife in the wild

5. Determining beetle abundance

6. Monitoring the effect of the insects on purple loosestrife populations

Although you can raise and release the insects in a few months during the spring, in order to follow their effect on purple loosestrife, students will need to monitor the plants over several years. Table 3.1 sets out is a timetable for the different steps in the purple loosestrife research project.

FIGURE 3.1
Purple Loosestrife

TABLE 3.1
Timetable for Purple Loosestrife Interactive Research Project

Time	Protocol
Year 1	
August–October	Conduct baseline plot sampling prior to releasing beetles.
Year 2	
March	Collect purple loosestrife root crown, place in pot in standing water. Allow 4–6 weeks for growth or until plants are 10–20 cm tall. Plants should be in sleeves or cages made out of mosquito netting.
Mid–late May	Add beetles (10–20 per plant). Allow 3–40 days for a new generation to appear. Optional: Survey purple loosestrife field site for presence of beetles.
Late June–early August	Release new generation of beetles.
August–October	Repeat plot sampling to determine effect of beetles.
Years 3–5	
Late May–early June	Survey for insect abundance and purple loosestrife growth.
August–October	Repeat plot sampling to determine effect of beetles.

NOTE: It is important that your research does not add to the purple loosestrife problem. Never transplant purple loosestrife into areas where it is not found already. At the end of the project, you and your teacher should return the plant parts to a site where purple loosestrife is already present.

Prior to starting your work, you will need to be able to identify purple loosestrife (Figure 3.1). Individual flowers have 5–6 pink or purple petals. The many individual flowers are at the top of stem, arranged in a "spike." Leaves are long and narrow. Two leaves are found across from each other on the stem, or there may be whorls of 3–4 leaves. Stems are woody and stiff, with 4–6 sides, rather than round. Mature plants grow up to 2 m tall. One root system can have 30–50 stems, thereby forming a large bushy cluster.

PART 1. BASELINE PLOT SAMPLING ON RELEASE SITE

This part of the protocol should be conducted in the late summer or early fall.

> **NOTE:** When working in the field it is good to wear eye protection to avoid being poked in the eye by stems.

Materials (for each plot)

- Quadrat frames
- Stakes to mark plots
- Permanent marker
- Plastic flagging
- Metric tape measure
- Ruler
- Copies of **Purple Loosestrife Data Form 1: Site Location** (pp. 139–140)
- Copies of **Purple Loosestrife Data Form 2: Fall Plot Sampling** (pp. 141–142)
- Map of the study site
- Camera
- Geographic Positioning System (GPS) (optional)

Procedure

1. Locate a site with purple loosestrife. Look for sites that

   - Are accessible for release and continued monitoring of beetles
   - Have at least 50 purple loosestrife plants, both mature and young, in a 10 m radius circle
   - Are sunny
   - Include a mixed plant community to allow other plants to recolonize once the purple loosestrife dies back

   Avoid sites that are subject to disturbances that might affect purple loosestrife or beetles (e.g., sites that are mowed, permanently flooded, treated with herbicides or insecticides, or where vandals are likely to remove your plot markers).

2. Get permission from the landowner to start a beetle release program on the site.

3. Mark the site on a county road map. You may want to use a GPS if available.

4. Describe the site location, environmental features, approximate number of purple loose-strife plants, and size of purple loosestrife patch using **Purple Loosestrife Data Form 1: Site Location**. Take a photograph of the site and mark the location from where you took the photo with a stake or flagging.

5. Sketch a map of the site on the **Purple Loosestrife Data Form 1: Site Location**. Note any features of the plot, such as lakes and roads.

6. Choose several locations in the purple loosestrife stand to sample the vegetation. If you wish to follow the protocol used by Cornell scientists, you will need a minimum of five sampling locations at the site. There are two ways to choose the sampling locations. For a site that is long and narrow, run a transect through the vegetation and select sampling locations at predetermined intervals (e.g., every 5, 10, or 20 meters). Alternatively, you can choose the locations using random or stratified sampling procedures (see Protocol 2). However, all plots must contain purple loosestrife. If necessary, shift the location of the plot so that purple loosestrife covers at least 30% of the plot.

7. Mark each location by hammering a piece of PVC pipe or other stake into the ground at one corner of the plot. The stake should be high enough to find again but short enough not to attract vandals. Mark the number of the site on the PVC pipe using permanent marker. Mark the plot numbers on the map you drew in step 5 above.

8. Lay out your quadrat frame and then permanently mark the other three corners of the 1 m² plot by hammering shorter pieces of pipe into the ground. Label each of the corners of the plot. Avoid stepping into the plot and minimize trampling around it.

9. Note any features of the plot, such as disturbance, flooding, and bird nests. Record this and other sampling data on the **Purple Loosestrife Data Form 2: Fall Plot Sampling**.

10. Estimate the percent of your plot covered by purple loosestrife and the percent covered by cattails. Cattails are a common wetland plant (Figure 3.2).

FIGURE 3.2
Cattails

11. Count the number of stems of purple loosestrife and of cattails.

12. Measure the height (in cm to the nearest 0.5 cm) of the five tallest stems of purple loosestrife and five tallest stems of cattails in your plot. As you locate each purple loosestrife stem, mark it with plastic flagging or in some other way so you can return to it to take other measurements.

13. Because the purple loosestrife beetles can affect the number of flower buds that produce seeds, it is important to collect information on the flowers. Count the total number of inflorescences on each of the five tallest purple loosestrife stems. An inflorescence is the portion of the stem from the lowest flower (or flower bud) to the end of the stem (Figure 3.3). Even if there is only one flower bud it is counted as one inflorescence. Also measure the total length of the longest inflorescence (from the lowest flower or bud to top of stem) to the nearest 0.5 cm on each of the five tallest stems.

FIGURE 3.3
Inflorescence

14. Collect the longest inflorescence from each of the five longest stems and place it in a plastic bag labeled with your plot number and the stem number. When back in the lab, cut a 5 cm piece from the center of each inflorescence and determine the number of flower buds per 5 cm (Figure 3.4).

FIGURE 3.4
Counting Flower Buds in a 5 cm Section of a Purple Loosestrife Inflorescence

15. Count the total number of purple loosestrife inflorescences in the sample plot.

16. Estimate the percent cover of the five most abundant plant species other than cattails or purple loosestrife. Use field guides to identify plant species.

17. *Optional*: List other plant species in the plot. If you cannot identify plants in the field, take a sample of the same plant from outside your plot and place it in a plastic bag labeled with your plot number. Using field guides and people knowledgeable about plant identification, try to identify the plants once you are back at school. Once you have identified a plant, you can make a herbarium collection to help students in other classes and in following years. You can make a customized list of common plants, with identification hints.

PART 2. GROWING PURPLE LOOSESTRIFE

Materials

▶ *Either* 4 gal pots with holes in the bottom, and minipond (e.g., children's swimming pool large enough to hold the 4 gal pots and with sides that are at least 1/4 the height of the 4 gal pots) *or* 4 gal pots with a plastic liner partially filled with water

▶ Shovels

▶ Wire tomato cages (one for each purple loosestrife plant)

▶ Twig clippers

▶ Branch clippers

▶ Plastic garbage bags

▶ String

▶ Duct tape

▶ Potting soil

▶ Fertilizer

▶ Posts

▶ String

Procedure

1. Purple loosestrife grows best under moist conditions. You can grow plants in pots that are lined with plastic or in pots with holes in the bottom that are placed in a tray or minipond. The number of purple loosestrife plants you intend to grow will determine the size of your minipond. For growing one or two plants indoors, a deep plant tray should suffice. For larger numbers of plants outdoors there are several options. A children's wading pool is a quick and easy way to set up a fairly large outdoor minipond. Make an overflow hole in the pool so that the level of water does not rise above 1/2 the height of the pot. Water too high after a rain could flood and/or tip over the pots. If you are growing a very large number of plants, you can construct a minipond with four pieces of 10 ft. long PVC pipe connected with elbows and covered with 20 mil black plastic.

2. Purple loosestrife plants can be collected from the field as soon as the ground thaws and softens in the spring. Collecting plants is usually a very muddy job, so dress appropriately and bring a change of clothing if headed back to school.

3. Use a shovel to loosen the root clump around several stems of purple loosestrife. Dig up roots of intermediate or smaller plants. Bigger ones are really tough and may be too big for your pots.

4. Cut all stems at ground level and place roots into a container or plastic bag so they won't dry out during transport. Transport back to school or other site where you will be growing purple loosestrife.

5. You also may need some purple loosestrife stems for backup in case the beetles eat all the leaves on the plants you are growing. Dig out an entire plant, including rootstock, and transport it to the lab. Then place the entire plant in a pot in the minipond and use its stems to feed the beetles if necessary.

6. Wash the root clump with a hose. Live, healthy root crowns are tan to brown in color. They are pink to white on the inside and somewhat flexible. Dead root crowns are black. Use the branch clipper to break the root clump into a size that will fit into your pots. Use the twig clipper to cut the dead stems to about 12 cm above the roots and trim off dead roots.

7. Fill the 4 gal pots 1/4 full of potting soil. Sprinkle in slow-release fertilizer 14–14–14. (Follow manufacturer's directions.)

8. Place one large or several small root crowns into the center of the pot. The side of the root crown where stems have been cut off should face up. Fill the pot with potting soil so that the plant is at the same depth it was in its original location. Pack the soil.

9. Put pots in the minipond. Be sure pots have holes in the bottom for water uptake. For the initial watering, water the plant from the top. From then on, keep the tray filled with water high enough to cover the lower 1/4 of the pots.

10. Place a tomato cage in the pot and press it all the way down. This will be used to hold up the mosquito netting sleeve around the plant (see p. 133).

11. If your plants are outdoors it is important to secure them so they do not blow over. Set up posts outside the minipond. Make a grid of string between the posts over the minipond and tie the tops of the sleeves to the grid.

12. If planting indoors, place the plant where it will receive the most light (a south-facing window). The temperature should be around 25ºC. If either sunlight or temperature is too low, use a grow light and/or heat light.

PART 3: RAISING PURPLE LOOSESTRIFE BEETLES

Introduction

Galerucella calmariensis is the Latin name for a beetle that eats purple loosestrife leaves. It is found throughout the range of purple loosestrife in Europe and Asia. The adults eat 1–2 mm holes in the leaves. In contrast, the larvae eat by scraping away the green leaf tissue from beneath leaving only the upper epidermis intact. The larvae also damage the buds that grow into flowers and shoots. When the beetle feeds on the leaves, the plant is not able to produce as many sugars through photosynthesis. The plant compensates for the loss of sugars by decreasing the production of new roots and shoots. This results in stunted plants. At high densities (2–3 larvae per cm of shoot), the beetle can destroy all the leaves of the plant.

If you raise *Galerucella* beetles (also called purple loosestrife beetles), you might want to know something about their life cycle. Understanding an insect's life cycle helps us to plan biological control programs. The *Galerucella* life cycle from egg to adult takes 30–40 days.

FIGURE 3.5
Adult *Galerucella* Beetle

Please note that the life cycle described here is typical for Ithaca, New York. Further south, beetles will become active earlier and further north, they stay in the litter (dead leaves on the top of the soil) longer. A good guide is the growth of purple loosestrife in the field. Once purple loosestrife stems are 5–10 cm tall, beetles will become active and can be found feeding on the plant. Find out about the detailed life cycle by talking to people who have released beetles in your area.

Adult beetles spend the winter in leaf litter. In the spring, they crawl out of the soil onto purple loosestrife. They first feed on the young tips and leaves of purple loosestrife. After a few days of feeding, they begin to reproduce. They lay most of their eggs in May and June but may continue laying eggs into July. Females lay masses of 2–18 eggs. A female may lay up to 400 eggs in one season.

FIGURE 3.6
Purple Loosestrife Beetle Eggs

About 4–7 days after the eggs are laid, the young larvae emerge. Young larvae feed mainly on young leaf and flower buds. Older larvae also feed on the leaves. Adults often fly to other plants when larvae begin to feed. After 3 weeks, larvae begin to pupate.

FIGURE 3.7
Purple Loosestrife Beetle Larva

Pupation occurs in the soil or leaf litter beneath the plant. If the water level is high the insects may pupate in the stem of the purple loosestrife around the level of the water line. New adults emerge in late June or early July, about 7–10 days after they pupated. Adults that emerge early in July may produce eggs the same year.

TABLE 3.1
Purple Loosestrife Beetle Life Cycle

May	May – July	August – May
Adults emerge from hibernation	Egg laying; larvae and new adults emerge	Adults overwinter

Materials

▶ Sleeve bags (constructed from mosquito netting, one per purple loosestrife plant)

▶ Aspirator (available from BioQuip)

▶ Purple loosestrife plants (see Part 2. Growing Purple Loosestrife, p. 130)

▶ *Galerucella* beetles, available through Cornell University Department of Natural Resources or local sources

▶ Elastic, duct tape, or string

▶ Garbage-bag ties

▶ Observation cage (optional)

Procedure

1. First construct gauze sleeve bags out of mosquito netting. Sew a cylinder of material, approximately 2 m tall, with a circumference to fit around the pots in which the purple loosestrife is growing.

2. You will need an aspirator to remove insects from the plants. Do not share an aspirator with another student unless it has been washed.

3. Next you will need a source of beetles. Contact the Cornell University Biological Control of Nonindigenous Plants program or check with your state or local natural resource agency.

4. When plants are about 20 cm tall, they are ready for the loosestrife beetles.

5. Put a sleeve over the plant. The tomato cage will hold the sleeves up.

6. Attach the bottom of the sleeve to the pot with elastic or by tying with string and duct taping to the top of the pot. It is very important to have a tight fit so that beetles do not escape.

7. Add 10–20 beetles to each pot. Be conservative. Beetles and the larvae they produce have a voracious appetite. Use a garbage-bag tie to close the top of the sleeve. Begin observations of insect activity. You can tell the insects are feeding when you see holes in leaves.

8. After 10 days, start checking the plants for eggs. Avoid opening the sleeve. Eggs are round and the size of a pinhead. They are white to cream in color. They are usually laid in groups with frass (feces) over them on leaves. Estimate the number of eggs that have been produced.

9. Leave the plants undisturbed for another 3 weeks so the larvae can develop. Larvae are yellow to orange with black stripes across their bodies. Larvae molt several times as they develop. Each growth stage between molts is called an *instar*. Early instars are hard to see. Full-grown larvae are 0.5 cm long.

10. Adults should begin to emerge and congregate at the top of the sleeve. Young beetles are light brown in color. Be careful that beetle populations do not get too high—the plant should never become totally defoliated. As an emergency measure you can place new stems in a cup of water and place in sleeve with original plant.

11. Collect adults for several days using an aspirator. Transfer adults to another sleeved plant with no beetles. Open the sleeve at the pot end and shake the beetles out of the aspirator. Reseal sleeve.

12. If you want to continue the project over several years, you can purchase new beetles each year. Alternatively, you can go back to the site where you released beetles the following May, and collect several beetles with an aspirator and repeat the process of raising them.

PART 4. RELEASING BEETLES

Introduction

The beetles that you release in late June will do most of their damage the next year. The larvae that follow can further reduce purple loosestrife populations. If you gathered baseline information about the area where you released the beetles, you can compare plant populations before and after releasing purple loosestrife beetles.

Materials

▶ Aspirator

▶ Purple loosestrife beetles

▶ Container to hold beetles *OR*

▶ Purple loosestrife plant with beetles in mosquito netting cage that you take into the field

Procedure

1. You can collect beetles for release using the aspirator. This allows you to get a count of how many beetles you are releasing. Alternatively, you can transport a purple loosestrife plant with its sleeve intact to the release site.

2. Once you have arrived at your field site, release the beetles from the aspirator or remove the sleeve. Allow the beetles to disperse.

PART 5. MONITORING INSECT POPULATIONS

You should monitor insect populations in the spring, starting the first year after you release the beetles.

Materials

▶ Quadrat frames

▶ Copies of **Purple Loosestrife Data Form 3: Insect Abundance** (p. 143)

▶ White sheet or plastic for collecting insects (optional)

▶ Ziploc plastic sandwich bags (optional)

Procedure

1. Return to the same sites you sampled prior to releasing the beetles.

2. Locate your plots. Be careful approaching the plants in your plots. Some beetles may drop off if they sense your approach or if you touch a stem.

3. Record on the **Purple Loosestrife Data Form 3: Insect Abundance** the time of day and weather conditions, as beetle activity may depend on temperature, cloudiness, etc.

4. Spend one minute searching for and recording the number of beetles of each life stage located. First count the number of adults found in one minute. (Look at the shoot tips.) Then count the number of eggs found in one minute. Then count the number of larvae found in one minute. Make sure not to step into the plot. This may be easiest to do if 2–3 students stand on different sides of the plot. Record your results on the **Purple Loosestrife Data Form 3: Insect Abundance.**

5. Describe any damage the insects have caused to the purple loosestrife plants in your plot.

6. *Optional*: Shake out a purple loosestrife plant over a sheet of cloth or plastic. Collect any insects that fall onto the sheet. Put these in Ziploc plastic bags with a piece of purple loosestrife for identification later when you return to school.

PART 6. MONITORING IMPACT OF BEETLES ON PURPLE LOOSESTRIFE POPULATIONS

1. In the spring when you monitor insect abundance (Part 5 above), locate the sampling plots, lay out the quadrat frames, and repeat steps 9–11 from Part 1. Baseline Plot Sampling. Enter your results on **Purple Loosestrife Data Form 4: Spring Plot Sampling** (p. 144). Also, take a photograph of the site from the same spot as in step 4 from Part 1. Baseline Plot Sampling (p. 127).

2. In early fall, relocate the sampling plots, lay out the quadrat frames, and then repeat steps 9–17 from Part 1. Baseline Plot Sampling. Use the same data form you used for the baseline sampling (**Purple Loosestrife Data Form 2: Fall Plot Sampling** p. 141). Also, take a photograph of the site from the same spot as in step 4 from Part 1. Baseline Plot Sampling (p. 127).

RELATED INTERACTIVE RESEARCH PROJECTS

Students and teachers may want to design other research projects focusing on purple loose-strife and biological control. We have provided some example research topics below but feel free to come up with your own ideas.

Success of Biological Control Programs

Not all biological control programs are successful. Sometimes insects do not reproduce and become established in the field. Or they may fail to disperse to new sites. Can you think of other reasons why biological control programs might fail? Following are some suggestions regarding factors you might want to consider in future research.

▶ Natural enemies of biological control agents (e.g., birds feeding on biocontrol insects)

▶ Number of insects needed to establish a population

▶ Weather conditions

▶ Time of year beetles are released

Host Specificity

The most important factor in choosing a biological control insect is whether it feeds only on the target plant. This is called *host specificity*. Can you imagine some of the impacts on plant populations, communities, and ecosystems if an introduced insect is not host specific? (See p. 26.)

Biocontrol scientists use screening tests to lower the risk of an introduced insect causing damage to other plants. They test to see if the insect feeds on plants that are related to the species they are trying to control. For example, if the plant they are trying to control is in the rose family, they would test the insect on other members of the rose family. Additionally, they would test the insect on other plants the insect might be likely to feed on, including plants on which the insect has been collected, plants that are eaten by insects related to the insect that is being introduced, plant species with similar morphology or biochemistry, and plants growing in the same habitat. They also test to see if the insect feeds on crops or ornamental plants of economic value. Usually 40–50 plant species are tested.

Operational Definitions and Quantifying Data

Scientists often have to come to agreement on how to measure things or how to define things. Operational definitions are ones that allow you to recognize something through its definition. For example, a calorie is the amount of energy needed to raise the temperature of one gram of water one degree Celsius.

The question of how to quantify test results is often an issue in research. In the case of host specificity, results should allow us to estimate how likely an insect is to shift to another host plant. How do we define a "safe" amount of host specificity?

One measure scientists use is that the insect should not be able to reproduce and should feed only minimally on a nontarget plant.

Screening tests should try to simulate natural conditions as closely as possible. This is so the results will most accurately predict what might happen in the field. Following are some types of screening tests.

▶ **No-choice test.** A single plant species is offered to the insect. No-choice tests can be used to eliminate the majority of test plants. If the insect does not eat the plant when no other food is available, the plant can be eliminated from further testing.

▶ **Multiple-choice test.** Several plant species, including the species you are hoping to control, are offered to the insect.

▶ **Field test cages.** These are large walk-in cages that allow plants to grow to their regular sizes. Normal habitat characteristics should be matched as closely as possible. A potential problem with field cages is that other insects may become trapped in the cage and also attack the plants or the biocontrol insects.

▶ **Open field tests.** These tests are closest to the actual release conditions and therefore most valid.

Scientists conducted host specificity tests for the beetle *Galerucella calmariensis* before they were allowed to release it in the U.S. and Canada. These tests were first performed in Germany (in the beetle's native range) before the beetle was allowed in the U.S. Once the beetle was brought to the U.S., the screening tests were done in quarantine. Scientists tested 44 species belonging to 16 plant families.

The scientists' findings included the following:

▶ In some of the no-choice tests, the beetles fed more and laid more eggs on the nontarget species than on purple loosestrife.

▶ Insects fed less and laid fewer eggs on nontarget plants when purple loosestrife was present and they could choose between the nontarget plant and purple loosestrife.

▶ Plants grown in a greenhouse or in quarantine developed different cell structures, as well as physiological anomalies, which could affect selection of these plants by the insects.

▶ Under open field conditions, insects fed less on nontarget plants than under lab and greenhouse conditions.

Validity vs. Control

Validity is how close your results are to what will really happen in nature. In some cases, experimental design itself can alter the test results. For example, insects in cages may feed on more plant species than they feed on in the field. Tests using entire potted plants will yield more valid test results than tests using just plant parts. Tests that include the host plant are generally more valid than those that only include species that are not targeted for control. Experiments that have conditions closest to those in the natural world often are most valid.

On the other hand, tests with conditions closest to what one finds in nature are generally not as well controlled as other experiments. Other insects may attack the target plant. Plants may die because of unusual weather conditions. Thus, often the most valid studies are the least controlled. Scientists often conduct a range of controlled and more natural experiments to solve an environmental problem. Because no one experiment gives all the answers, scientists piece together evidence from multiple studies.

Ideas for possible investigations include

▶ Comparing feeding of purple loosestrife beetles on purple loosestrife and other local plants

▶ Comparing insect feeding on leaves and flowers cut off from plants compared to leaves and flowers in potted plants

▶ Conducting no-choice and multiple-choice tests

▶ Observing whether purple loosestrife biocontrol beetles are found resting or feeding on other species besides purple loosestrife after they are released in the field

You can purchase small observation cages to test whether beetles feed on leaves, flowers, and other plant parts. Alternatively, you can use the pots with sleeves for tests on whole plants.

A more ambitious study would involve field test cages. These can be constructed by making a 4 m x 4 m x 2 m high cage out of PVC pipe. Luminite is a strong covering material. The large field cages can double as large breeding cages if you wish to expand your release program.

Open field tests are most useful in predicting what may happen in the field but may open the study to too many variables. For example, if unusual weather prevails, it may be difficult to determine whether results are due to weather or beetles.

Purple Loosestrife Populations

How widespread is purple loosestrife in your community? You can map the location of purple loosestrife in your school district. Each student can look for purple loosestrife within 1 km of his or her home. Include location, approximate number of plants, and plant density on your map. Base maps may be obtained from government natural resources agencies, outdoor stores, bus garages, school districts, or Cooperative Extension.

PURPLE LOOSESTRIFE DATA FORM 1: SITE LOCATION

Fill out one form for each area with purple loosestrife plants.

Name(s) _____

School _____

School address _____

Teacher's name _____

Phone _____ Email _____

Site name _____

4.* Location of purple loosestrife

Nearest city or town _____

County _____

State _____

Name of lake or stream (if applicable) _____

Nearest road intersection _____

4.* Type of area (check one)

❏ Wetland   ❏ Pond or lake   ❏ Stream or river

❏ Ditch   ❏ Meadow or pasture

❏ Other (specify)

4.* Number of purple loosestrife plants in area (check one)

❏ < 20   ❏ 20–99   ❏ 100–999   ❏ > 1000

4.* Size of purple loosestrife patch (check one)

❏ 1 m²   ❏ 1–100 m²   ❏ > 100 m²

---

*Numbers refer to steps in **Baseline Plot Sampling on Release Site** procedure, p. 127.

PURPLE LOOSESTRIFE DATA FORM 1 *(continued)*

5.* Sketch a map of area where purple loosestrife is found below.

Show roads, natural features such as lakes, distances if possible, and an outline of the purple loosestrife patch.

7.* Show locations of quadrats along with quadrat number on the map.

---

*Numbers refer to steps in **Baseline Plot Sampling on Release Site** procedure, starting on p. 127.

PURPLE LOOSESTRIFE DATA FORM 2: FALL PLOT SAMPLING

Fill out one form for each plot before and after beetle release. Use for late summer or fall sampling.

Name(s) _____

School _____

Teacher's name _____● _____

Date (include year) _____

Before or after beetle release (check one)   ❏ Before   ❏ After

Plot # _____

Site name _____

9.* Describe any features of plot (recent flooding, bird nests, insects, etc.)

10.* Percent cover of purple loosestrife and cattail

Plant species	Percent cover					
	0%	1–5%	6–25%	26–50%	51–75%	76–100%
Purple loosestrife						
Cattail						

11.* Number of stems of purple loosestrife and cattail

Plant species	Number of stems
Purple loosestrife	
Cattail	

---

*Numbers refer to steps in **Baseline Plot Sampling on Release Site** procedure, starting on p. 127.

PURPLE LOOSESTRIFE DATA FORM 2 *(continued)*

12.* Height of five tallest cattail plants

Plant #	Height (cm)
1	
2	
3	
4	
5	

12, 13, and 15.* Height and inflorescences of five tallest purple loosestrife

Plant # *Procedure Step*	Height (cm) *12*	Inflorescences per plant (#) *13*	Length of longest inflorescence (cm) *13*	Flower buds per 5 cm (#) *14*
1				
2				
3				
4				
5				

15.* Total number of purple loosestrife inflorescences in plot: _____

16.* Percent cover of five most abundant species besides purple loosestrife and cattail

Plant species	Percent cover					
	0%	1–5%	6–25%	26–50%	51–75%	76–100%
1						
2						
3						
4						
5						

17.* List other plants in quadrat

---

*Numbers refer to steps in **Baseline Plot Sampling on Release Site** procedure, starting on p. 127.

PURPLE LOOSESTRIFE DATA FORM 3: INSECT ABUNDANCE

Fill out one form for each plot during spring after beetle release.

Name(s) _____

School _____

Teacher's name _____

Date (include year) _____

Site name _____

3.* Time of day _____

3.* Weather conditions _____

_____

Plot # _____

Date beetles were released _____

4.* One minute beetle counts

Number of adults found per minute _____

Number of eggs found per minute _____

Number of larvae found per minute _____

5.* How much damage was done to the purple loosestrife?

6.* Other insects found on purple loosestrife (optional).

_____

*Numbers refer to steps in **Monitoring Insect Populations** procedure, p. 135.

PURPLE LOOSESTRIFE DATA FORM 4: SPRING PLOT SAMPLING

Fill out one form for each plot after beetle release. Use for spring sampling.

Name(s) _____

School _____

Teacher's name _____

Date (include year) _____

Plot # _____

Site name _____

9. * Describe any features of quadrat (recent flooding, bird nests, insects, etc.)

10. * Percent cover of purple loosestrife and cattail

Plant species	Percent cover					
	0%	1–5%	6–25%	26–50%	51–75%	76–100%
Purple loosestrife						
Cattail						

11. * Number of stems of purple loosestrife and cattail

Plant species	Number of stems
Purple loosestrife	
Cattail	

---

*Numbers refer to steps in **Baseline Plot Sampling on Release Site** procedure, starting on p. 127.

PHRAGMITES PROJECTS

PHRAGMITES INSECT SURVEY— BACKGROUND

The common reed, *Phragmites australis*, is found on every continent except Antarctica. It is undoubtedly one of the most widely distributed plant species in the world. It grows in a variety of wetlands, including alongside streams, ponds, and roadside ditches, and in tidal and freshwater marshes.

Archaeologists have found *Phragmites* in 3000-year-old peat cores from tidal marshes in Connecticut. It also has been found in mats and other woven objects at Anasazi sites in southwestern Colorado, dating from 600–900 A.D.

Thus, similar to white-tailed deer, *Phragmites* is a native North American species. However, in the early 1800s, an aggressive variety of *Phragmites* was introduced to North America from Europe. The European strains outcompete native North American *Phragmites* and have become invasive in much of the Northeast and Midwest. It is possible that environmental changes (e.g., nutrient runoff into wetlands) also have been responsible for *Phragmites* becoming invasive, similar to how changes in habitat have allowed deer populations to expand dramatically.

Similar to many other invasives, introduced *Phragmites* often outcompetes native wetland species, and in some cases may be causing local extinctions of rare plants. Populations of waterfowl and other wildlife that depend on native vegetation have declined where *Phragmites* has invaded.

FIGURE 3.8
Phragmites australis

Phragmites is a tall grass that grows up to 4.5 m tall and lives for many years. Once it reaches a site, it spreads primarily by growth of horizontal below-ground stems called rhizomes. New shoots emerge from these rhizomes and the plant continues to spread. Each group of shoots growing from one "mother" plant is called a clone, because the shoots are genetically identical.

Land managers and scientists are experimenting with different ways of controlling *Phragmites*, including mowing, spraying herbicides, and changing water levels. In addition, Dr. Bernd Blossey and colleagues at Cornell University are in the initial stages of developing a biological control program for *Phragmites*.

The first step in a biological control program is to learn about the ecology of the pest plant and its herbivores. Thus, scientists are conducting studies to learn more about where *Phragmites* is found and what insects are growing on it. They have discovered at least 20 species of non-native insects living on *Phragmites* in the U.S. These insects were accidentally introduced to North America from Europe. Most of them have been observed first near New York City, where ships constantly arrive from Europe sometimes carrying insect and other unintended "hitchhikers." Similar to other invasive species (for example, the chestnut blight, see p. 7) the insects are spreading west from New York City.

Scientists hope that some of these insects may eventually become part of a biocontrol program to halt *Phragmites* invasions. To evaluate whether this is possible, they need to collect a lot of information about the insects. Questions scientists currently are researching include:

▶ What types of insects are currently found on *Phragmites* in North America?

▶ What is the distribution of these insects within North America?

▶ Where do these insects prefer to live within a patch of *Phragmites,* and on single *Phragmites* plants?

▶ How do weed control treatments such as herbicides and burning affect the insects?

Collecting and identifying the insects currently living on *Phragmites* is an important first step in understanding what further efforts are necessary to develop a biological control program. Some of this information can be collected using the protocols below. You may want to share what you have learned with Cornell scientists. You also can design your own research projects to address some of the questions above or questions you come up with on your own.

PHRAGMITES INTERACTIVE RESEARCH

Many insects overwinter as larvae in the stalks of *Phragmites*. They may be found by dissecting plants during the fall and winter months. Swiss scientist Patrick Häfliger has developed a key to the larvae and feeding damage of insects found on *Phragmites*. Information about the insects and how to identify them, including larval color, how far up the stems they are found, and the shape of the galls or tunnels they construct in *Phragmites* stems, is available on the Web.

Because these insects are difficult to identify, the key includes not only color and other characteristics of the larvae, but also information about their living habits. For example, the key includes information on the shape of the galls or tunnels that insects construct in *Phragmites* stems and on how far up the stems they are found.

It is important to take good notes and handle stems carefully when dissecting plants in order not to destroy information that could help in identifying the insects. While you may not be able to identify each insect, it is extremely helpful if you can recognize differences between them and place them in different groups.

Unlike much ecological research, which is carried out during the summer growing season, *Phragmites* insects are collected in winter while they are overwintering inside the stems (October to

SCi LINKS.
THE WORLD'S A CLICK AWAY

Topic: invasive species
Go to: www.sciLINKS.org
Code: IE01

February are good times to sample many *Phragmites* insects). You can simply gather *Phragmites* stems from a nearby wetland and observe and identify the insects found in the stems (see **Dissecting the Stems** procedure on p. 150). Please dispose of stems close to where you gather them so as not to spread *Phragmites* and the insects.

If you are interested in answering questions about the distribution of the insects in your region and within the individual stands of *Phragmites*, and even sharing your data with scientists, then you will need to follow additional sampling protocols (see **Stand Description and Sampling** procedure, p. 148). Some groups may want to share the information they collect with Cornell scientists. The Cornell scientists studying *Phragmites* only have enough time and money to collect data from a limited number of sites. However, to understand *Phragmites* ecology, it is important to have data from as many sites and over as large a region as possible. You likely will work at a site the scientists haven't visited and thus can add to our overall understanding of the ecology of *Phragmites* and associated insects. If you want to share your data with Cornell, please access the Cornell University *Phragmites* website *www.invasiveplants.net/phragmites* prior to sampling to find out more details on recent protocols and data reporting.

Observational Studies

You may have heard that every scientific experiment has to have experimental treatments and a control treatment. However, not all work that scientists do requires a treatment and a control. The *Phragmites* protocol is an observational study, which means that you are recording data about the natural world without modifying anything. Often ecologists conduct observational studies before engaging in a controlled experiment. This gives them important background information that they then can use in designing an experiment.

For example, let's say that you learn, through an observational study like the one we describe here, that a particular type of insect only lives in *Phragmites* at the top of a stem. You might then ask a question: Why do they only live at the top of stems? You might have some ideas about the answer to your question, which you can formulate into a hypothesis. Maybe they live at the tops because the stems are not so thick at the top, and it is easier to bore through the stems there. A controlled experiment could then be designed to determine whether the insect is capable of laying eggs through a thicker layer of stem. (Perhaps you could put insects in cages with stems of different thicknesses and you could observe whether they lay more eggs in the thinner stems.)

Notice that observations are made in all scientific studies. What makes an observational study unique is that no treatments are imposed, and therefore, no control treatment is necessary.

PART 1. STAND DESCRIPTION AND SAMPLING

NOTE: Skip to Part 2. **Collecting Stems** if you want to just look for insects.

Materials

▶ Compass

▶ Topographic or road map of area

▶ Meter sticks

▶ 1 m x 1 m quadrat frame

▶ Metric measuring tape or brightly colored, nonstretch, durable string and duct tape

▶ Brightly colored flagging

▶ Permanent markers (sharpies)

▶ Pruners

▶ Large, heavy bags for plants

▶ Clipboard, paper, and pencil (for mapping *Phragmites* patch and drawing location of samples)

▶ Safety goggles

▶ Boots (if sampling in water)

▶ Work gloves

▶ Copies of *Phragmites* **Data Form 1: Site Description** (pp. 154–155)

▶ Copies of *Phragmites* **Data Form 2: Sampling Plots** (p. 156)

NOTE: Students should wear solid shoes, long sleeves and pants, and eye protection. Walking through a *Phragmites* stand can be difficult.

Procedure

1. Locate a site with *Phragmites*. Look for sites that are accessible and have at least 50 *Phragmites* stems in a 10 m radius.

2. Get permission from the landowner to conduct research on the site.

3. Mark the site on a county road map or topographic map.

4. Describe the site location, type of site, and approximate number of *Phragmites* plants using the *Phragmites* **Data Form 1: Site Description**. Take a photograph of the site. Mark the site where you take the photograph with a stake so you can return to take photos later on.

5. On the *Phragmites* **Data Form 1: Site Description**, make an outline sketch of the shape of the *Phragmites* stand. Include any prominent features such as roads and ponds. Try to estimate the size of the overall stand.

6. If you will be using a string to lay out your transect, you need to mark off the intervals at which you will be placing your sampling quadrats (e.g., every 5 or 10 m). Tie one end of the string to a fixed object and stretch the string out. Wrap duct tape around the string at the set intervals, and label the distance from the beginning of the string. After marking 50–100 m of string, rewind the string.

7. Tie plastic (forestry) flagging to a *Phragmites* stem at the edge of the stand. This will mark the beginning of your sampling transect.

8. Run a transect (metric tape or marked string) through the *Phragmites* stand and select sampling locations at predetermined intervals (e.g., every 5, 10, or 20 m). Go straight through the vegetation without veering to the left or right. Depending on the size of the *Phragmites* stand, it is best to have between five and ten 1 m^2 plots spaced evenly along the transect. If time is limited, you can sample one plot and come back later to sample others.

9. Note the orientation of your transect and draw the transect on the sketch of the *Phragmites* stand.

10. At each sampling location, tie brightly colored flagging to the nearest *Phragmites* stem. The stem will be the corner of the plot. Write the plot number on the flagging using permanent marker.

11. Lay out your quadrat frame.

12. Note any features of the plot, such as disturbance, flooding, bird nests, bare soil, and leaf litter. Record data on **Phragmites Data Form 2: Sampling Plots.**

13. Count the number of stems of *Phragmites* in your 1 m^2 sampling plot. Record data on **Phragmites Data Form 2: Sampling Plots.**

PART 2. COLLECTING STEMS

Materials

❭ Pruners

❭ Large, heavy bags for plants

❭ Duct tape

❭ Scotch tape

❭ Markers

❭ Labels

❭ Goggles

❭ Work gloves

Note of Caution

Be careful when handling the *Phragmites* shoots because the ends of the cut shoots can be sharp. Broken *Phragmites* stems can be dangerous to work with. If you bend over and do not notice a stem, you may poke your eye with the shoot and damage your vision. Students should wear solid shoes or boots, long sleeves and pants, gloves, and eye protection.

Procedure

1. Using the pruners, cut all the tan shoots in the plot at the soil surface. (If you are not using a plot, cut 25 tan stems.) Tan shoots are this year's growth whereas gray stems are from last year. If you are unsure of which shoots to cut, then cut them all. If the area is flooded, cut the shoots at the water surface.

2. Bundle all the stems from each plot together with duct tape and mark the plot number on the duct tape. This way you will know where each bundle of *Phragmites* came from within the stand, which is useful if you are sharing data with Cornell or conducting studies beyond simply identifying insects.

3. If plants are too tall to transport or put into bags, fold each stem individually before bundling it with others in its plot. Use scotch tape to tie pieces of the same stem together so they don't break and become separated.

4. Cut the seed heads off from the tops of the plants and leave them at the site where the stems were collected. This prevents further distributing *Phragmites* to other locations. Label shoots to distinguish which were flowering and which were not. If any flowering parts seem strange in appearance, such as having a compacted flower head, save these parts and label where they came from. These differences might be caused by insect damage, and it is important to note them.

5. Store the stems outside. If you need to store stems inside, do the dissections for the insects as soon as possible after you collect the stems. Insects will emerge from the stems in a warm classroom.

PART 3. DISSECTING THE STEMS

Materials

▸ Small dull-bladed pocket knives or scissors

▸ Cups and paper towels for keeping insects

▸ Sandwich bags (for keeping galls or other plant parts)

▸ Hand lens

▸ Calipers

▸ Drawing paper (for sketching, describing different insects)

▸ Meter sticks or tape measures

▸ Copies of *Phragmites* **Data Form 3: Insects** (p. 157)

Procedure

1. Beginning with stems from the first plot, number each stem consecutively as you remove it from the bundle.

2. Notice whether there are any breaks in the stem. Even if you folded it, look at the points where you broke it. Sometimes the stem breaks more easily at points where insects have attacked.

3. Note whether there is any bird damage to the stem. Holes from birds are generally larger than those made by emerging insects. In addition, if you have the current year's stems, no insects should have yet emerged. Record your observations on **Phragmites Data Form 3: Insects.**

4. Note whether the stem was flowering.

5. Measure the stem length using the meter stick.

6. Measure the stem diameter at the base of the stem using calipers (Figure 3.9).

7. Starting at the bottom of the stem, split the stem open using the knife or scissors. Do not slice through it completely in a way that would injure the insects that might be living inside. Some species are small and difficult to spot. Be careful not to overlook these or the ones in the shoot tips. On plants that have not flowered often we find larvae living in the shoot tips. These are called shoot tip flies. Occasionally the tips form a gall (hard tissue with larger diameter than the stem) and the larva is found inside. Continue splitting the stem open (you may be able to pull it apart after starting it with the knife or scissors).

8. If you find an insect, stop splitting the stem and record data about the insect as follows:

   a. Each time you see an insect, give it a name and note the finding on the **Phragmites** Data Form 3: Insects. When you see an insect that you or others in your class have not seen before, share your finding with the class and come up with a name that will be used for this insect (e.g., small yellow pupa).

   b. Note whether the insect is found in the top, middle, or bottom third of the stem.

   c. Notice any other organisms or structures that might be present where the insects are present (such as fungi, galls, etc.).

   d. Draw the insect as it looks in the stem.

   e. Once all data about an insect have been recorded, you can try to identify it using the online guide (see pg. 147). Record the name of the insect on the data form.

   f. To study the insect in more detail, you can put the insect on a moist paper towel in a cup and wait for it to complete development. This is a great opportunity to learn about insect life cycles.

9. Summarize the data for each insect on the **Phragmites** Data Form 3: Insects. Include the number of times it was found, where on the stem it was commonly found, and what organisms and structures it was commonly associated with. You do not need to count every insect, because often a group of larvae are found together and it is difficult to count them.

10. If no insects are found, or if you have completed recording findings on your data sheet, go back to step 1 and dissect another stem. Insects will not be present in every stem, and you may dissect many stems before you find any insects.

Figure 3.9

Measuring *Phragmites* Stem Diameter

Stem Disposal

Phragmites stalks should be disposed of in the school dumpster or put back where they were collected. If you have cut off the seed heads in the field, you can compost stems along with other schoolyard waste, but they will take a long time to decompose.

Data Analysis and Interpretation

Use the data on the table with the names of the insects and how often you encountered them to construct a bar graph of insect frequency. Which insects were most common? Did the different insects occupy different locations on the stems? Did they form characteristic galls that might be recognized from the outside of the stem?

If you sampled several different plots, look for differences across the plots. For each plot on the map, record the total number of times you encountered insects. Do plots at the edge of the *Phragmites* patch have more or fewer insects than those in the center? Do plots near the road have more or fewer insects than those away from the road? Do the plots differ in what insect species are found in them? Can you come up with any reasonable hypotheses for any differences you find? Then, repeat these questions using total numbers of each insect species separately (instead of all insects combined). Do different insects occupy different areas of the stand?

You may want to graph stem diameter or height against the number of times a given species of insect was encountered. Stem diameter or stem heights should be on the x-axis, and the number of times insects were encountered should be on the y-axis.

RELATED INTERACTIVE RESEARCH TOPICS

Now that you know how to sample and dissect *Phragmites* stems and identify the insects, you may have research questions of your own that you want to follow up on. We have included some example research projects below, but feel free to come up with your own ideas and discuss them with your teacher.

Bird Studies

Scientists and bird watchers are beginning to observe that birds seem to be following the insects that are colonizing *Phragmites*. The downy woodpecker, black-capped chickadee, and tufted titmouse have been observed feeding on some of the organisms that attack *Phragmites*.

▶ What birds can you observe in patches of *Phragmites*?

▶ Do they appear to be feeding on the insects?

▶ If so, do they make characteristic holes in the stems that can be used as evidence that birds have been feeding on stems?

▶ In stands where you find more insects, do you also find more birds?

Vegetation Studies

Are the species of plants found in *Phragmites* patches different from those found in other wetlands? You may want to sample vegetation in patches of *Phragmites* and in patches of other wetland plants using plots.

However, the results of such a survey will not show what is causing any differences in plant communities. This is because you have no way of knowing whether the *Phragmites* colonized this site because other plants were not doing well or if other plants are not doing well because *Phragmites* invaded the site. Alternatively, any patterns you find might be due partly to chance—that is, whether or not seeds of *Phragmites* or other plants reached the site.

Such surveys can lead you to questions that can be investigated further. For example, if you find plant species that are found only in wetlands where *Phragmites* is not present, you might want to design further studies, such as cutting down the *Phragmites* and seeing if the other plants establish on the site.

Distribution

▶ Is *Phragmites* expanding or declining in your area? You could conduct a regional survey and develop a baseline map showing locations of *Phragmites* in your area. Future students could follow the patches you identified and identify any new patches.

▶ Are there any patterns that might help explain *Phragmites* distribution? (E.g., are patches found along roadsides that are disturbed by mowing? Are there patches along roadsides that might be affected by salt that has been applied to melt snow and ice?)

▶ Are there any factors that might explain changes in populations of *Phragmites*? (E.g., decreased use of road salt? Increasing insect populations on *Phragmites*?)

PHRAGMITES DATA FORM 1: SITE DESCRIPTION

Fill out one form for each area with Phragmites plants.

Name(s) _____

School _____

School address _____

Teacher's name _____

Phone _____ Email _____

Site name _____

3.* Location of *Phragmites*

Nearest city or town _____

County _____ State _____

Name of lake or stream (if applicable) _____

Nearest road intersection _____

3.* Type of area (check one)

❑ Wetland   ❑ Pond or lake   ❑ Stream or river

❑ Ditch   ❑ Meadow or pasture

❑ Other (specify)

4.* Number of *Phragmites* plants in area (check one)

❑ < 20   ❑ 20–99   ❑ 100–999   ❑ > 1000

5.* Size of *Phragmites* patch (check one)

❑ 1 m²   ❑ 1–100 m²   ❑ > 100 m²

_____

*Numbers refer to steps in **Stand Description and Sampling** procedure, p. 148.

PHRAGMITES DATA FORM 1 *(continued)*

5.* Sketch a map of area where *Phragmites* is found below.

Show roads, natural features such as lakes, distances if possible, and an outline of the *Phragmites* patch.

9.* Show locations of transect and sampling plots on the map.

PHRAGMITES DATA FORM 2: SAMPLING PLOTS

Please fill out one form for each plot where you collect Phragmites.

Name(s) _____

School _____

Teacher's name _____

Date (include year) _____

Site name _____

Plot # _____

12. * **Describe any features of plot (e.g., recent flooding, bird nests, insects).**

13. * **Number of stems in your 1 m² plot**

*Numbers refer to steps in **Stand Description and Sampling** procedure, starting on p. 148.

NATIONAL SCIENCE TEACHERS ASSOCIATION

PHRAGMITES DATA FORM 3: INSECTS

Fill out one form for each Phragmites stem you dissect.

Name(s) _____

School _____

Teacher's name _____

Date (include year) _____

Site name _____

Plot # _____

Stem # _____

3.* Describe any evidence of bird damage.

4.* Stem flowering ☐ Yes ☐ No

5.* Stem length _____ m

6.* Stem diameter at base _____ mm

8.* Each time you encounter an insect, fill out the following information.

Insect name given by class 8a*	Insect name according to identification key 8e*	Where found on stem (bottom, middle, top third) 8b*	Organisms/ structures present (e.g., fungi, galls) 8c*

*Numbers refer to steps in **Dissecting the Stems** procedure, starting on p. 150.

PHRAGMITES DATA FORM 3 *(continued)*

9.* Summary data on insects

Insect name	Number of times insect encountered on stem	Where most often found on stem (bottom, middle, top)	Organisms/structures commonly associated with insect (e.g., fungi, galls)

8d.* Use the space below and extra sheets to sketch insects encountered.

Insect name

Insect name

Insect name

---

*Numbers refer to steps in **Dissecting the Stems** procedure, starting on p. 150.

INTERACTIVE
RESEARCH FORMS

Ask your teacher where each of these forms fits in the Environmental Inquiry
research process.

CHOOSING A RESEARCH TOPIC

Name _____ Date _____

What invasive species are beginning to enter our area?

Where is species x found in our local nature preserve?

Do species differ in sites with and without purple loosestrife?

Are there invasive species in our local wetlands?

Do sites with garlic mustard have different soil decomposition rates than sites with no garlic mustard?

What plants colonize wetlands after purple loosestrife is controlled by beetles?

1. Make a list of questions you would be interested in investigating using the ecology protocols.

   Example: What plants colonize wetlands after purple loosestrife is controlled by beetles?

NATIONAL SCIENCE TEACHERS ASSOCIATION

2. Of these questions, which seem the most important and interesting? Pick three:

   1.

   2.

   3.

3. For each of the three questions you have chosen, think of how you might design a research project. Then fill out this form:

Potential Questions

Question	Brief description of research you might do to address this question	What equipment and supplies would you need?	How long would it take to carry out this project?	Would fieldwork or travel to field sites be required?
Example: What plants colonize wetlands after purple loosestrife is controlled by beetles?	*Conduct plot sampling in sites where beetles have been released and compare to sites where they were not released.*	*Quadrat stakes for making permanent plots.*	*You would have to follow the plots for several years after the beetles were released.*	*Fieldwork is required. Travel time to site is ...hours.*
Question 1:				
Question 2:				
Question 3:				

4. Looking over your questions, consider whether each project would be feasible for you to carry out. Are the equipment and supplies available? Do you have enough time? Are there other students or interested people available to help? Will you be able to do whatever fieldwork is needed? Eliminate any questions that do not seem feasible based on logistics such as these.

	Would this project be feasible?	Why or why not?
Example Project	<u>Yes</u> No	*We have a site in our county where purple loosestrife beetles were released 3 years ago and other similar sites where they were not released. The park ranger where they were released is willing to help us with the fieldwork.*
Project 1	Yes No	
Project 2	Yes No	
Project 3	Yes No	

5. Choose a project you have decided is feasible and interesting and then continue on to the **Interactive Research Planning Form #1 or #2.**

INTERACTIVE RESEARCH PLANNING FORM 1

(for early detection surveys and beginning/exploratory level experiments)

Name _____ Date _____

1. **What question have you chosen to investigate, and why?**

   Example: What invasive species are present in the roadside ditch next to our school? If we find out what is there, maybe we can develop a means to control the unwanted species and plant native species.

2. **Briefly describe a project you would like to do to address this question.**

   Example: We will become familiar with the wetland native and non-native, invasive species in your region and how to identify them using the Web and field guides. Then we will go out to the ditch and record what species we find. We will need to be careful to stay on the path next to the ditch and not go on the road.

3. **What supplies will you need? How will you get any that are not already available in your classroom?**

   Example: We will need field guides from the library and data forms.

INTERACTIVE RESEARCH PLANNING FORM 1 *(continued)*

4. **How do you plan to schedule your project?**

   Example: It will be best to do this toward the end or beginning of the school year when the plants are easier to recognize.

5. **Can you find reports by other students or professional scientists on this topic? If so, what can you learn from what has already been done?**

6. **Meet with another student or group to discuss these plans using the Research Design Peer Review Form (p. 174). Then describe any changes you've decided to make based on this discussion.**

INTERACTIVE RESEARCH PLANNING FORM 2

(for rigorously designed experiments)

Name _____ Date _____

1. **What question do you plan to investigate?**

   Example: What is the effect of earthworms on decomposition in forest soils?

2. **Why is this question important or relevant to environmental issues?**

   Example: Earthworms from Europe and Asia are invading forest soils in the northeastern U.S. Some scientists think that they may be increasing the rate of decomposition, which could cause excess nitrogen, in the form of nitrate, to be washed out of the soil. Nitrates cause contamination of lakes and groundwater.

3. **Can you find reports by other students or professional scientists on this topic? If so, what can you learn from what has already been done?**

4. **What is your hypothesis (the prediction of what you think will happen, stated in a way that can be tested by doing an experiment)? Why did you choose this prediction?**

   Example: Soil decomposition rates will be higher in soils with earthworms than in soils without earthworms.

INTERACTIVE RESEARCH PLANNING FORM 2 *(continued)*

5. **What is your independent variable** (the factor that you will change to make one treatment different from another)?

   Example: Presence or absence of earthworms.

6. **What is your dependent variable?** (This is the factor you will measure to determine the results of the experiment. It is called "dependent" because the results depend on changes in the independent variable from one treatment to the next.)

   Example: CO_2 production, which is an indication of how fast organic matter in soils is decomposing.

> If you are confused about the independent and dependent variables, it may help to think back to your research question and then think about how you might want to present the results of your experiment. For example, for a microcosm experiment with earthworms and soil, you might set up a graph that looks something like the one below before you've entered the data.
>
> On the x-axis is your independent variable. This is the factor that you change.
>
> On the y-axis is your dependent variable. This is the factor you will be measuring in your experiment, such as CO_2 production in soils.

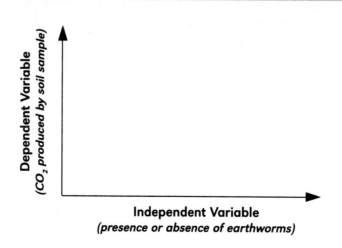

INTERACTIVE RESEARCH PLANNING FORM 2 *(continued)*

7. What **treatments** do you plan? (Each level of your independent variable is a treatment. You should plan to change only the independent variable from one treatment to the next, keeping all other conditions constant.)

   Example: In this experiment, I have only one treatment—presence of earthworms. I could have several treatments, such as different numbers of earthworms added to each soil sample.

8. How many **replicates** will you have for each treatment? (These are groups of organisms that are exposed to exactly the same conditions. The more replicates you can manage, the better, but you will have to figure out how many are possible with the supplies and time you have available.)

   Example: I can handle 5 replicates for each treatment.

9. What is your **control** (the untreated group that serves as a standard of comparison)?

   Example: Soils with no worms is the control. The microcosms in the control group will be exposed to all the same conditions as the microcosms in the treatment groups, except for the one variable I am testing (presence of earthworms).

10. What factors will you keep **constant** for all treatments? (The constants in an experiment are all the factors that do not change.)

    Examples: Temperature or light.

INTERACTIVE RESEARCH PLANNING FORM 2 *(continued)*

11. **What equipment and supplies will you need?**

12. **What schedule will you follow? Think about how many days will be needed for your experiment.**

13. **What will you measure, and how will you display your data? Sketch an empty data table here, with the appropriate headings. (Think about what kind of table you will need to record the data from your experiment.)**

On this graph, add labels for the x-axis and y-axis and sketch your expected results.

INTERACTIVE RESEARCH PLANNING FORM 2 *(continued)*

A Final Check: Evaluate Your Experimental Design

1. Does your planned experiment actually test your *hypothesis*?

2. Are you changing only one *variable* at a time? Which one?

3. Will your *control* be exposed to exactly the same conditions as your *treatment*s (except for the *independent variable*)?

4. How many *replicates* will you have for each *treatment*?

5. Meet with another student or group to discuss these plans using the **Research Design Peer Review Form** (p. 174). Then describe any changes you've decided to make based on this discussion.

RESEARCH REPORT FORM

Name _____ Date _____

1. What is the title of your research project?

2. What is your research question? Why is this question significant to environmental or other real-world issues?

3. Summarize what others have found out about this question.

4. What species did you use?

5. What sites did you work at or get your samples from?

6. Summarize your procedures here.

RESEARCH REPORT FORM *(continued)*

7. Summarize your data in a table. Column 1 should have the different levels of your independent variable (e.g., worms, no worms). Column 2 should list the replicate number for each level of the independent variable. Column 3 should have the data for your dependent variable (e.g., CO_2 levels measured). Additional columns may be needed if there were several dependent variables, to record moisture content or value of blank samples, etc. You will need to modify the table if your research was not an experiment.

Levels of independent variable	Replicate #	Responses of dependent variable

8. If you had replicates, determine the average of all replicates for each treatment level.

9. Graph and then summarize your data. What is your interpretation of the meaning of these results?

RESEARCH REPORT FORM *(continued)*

10. What conclusions can you reach? (What did you learn from your research? Can you think of any other possible explanations for your results?)

11. If you looked into the research that others may have done on this subject, how do your results agree or disagree with what they found?

12. If you were to repeat the research, what would you change in order to learn more about the question you studied? (Did you come up with any questions you couldn't answer using your data? Can you think of a research project that would help to answer these questions?)

13. What might you change to improve your research design?

POSTER DESIGN GUIDELINES

Posters are one way in which scientists present their research results. When posters are displayed at conferences, researchers have the opportunity to discuss their findings and ideas with fellow scientists.

At a poster session, people tend to spend the most time looking at posters that are attractive, well organized, and easy to read. It's best to keep the text short and to illustrate your points with graphs, photos, and diagrams.

To make your poster effective, make sure that it is

Readable—Can your text be read from 2 meters away? (20 point is a good font size.)

Understandable—Do your ideas fit together and make sense?

Organized—Is your work summarized clearly, using the headings listed in the example below?

Attractive—Will your poster make viewers want to take the time to read it? Have you used illustrations and color to enhance your display, without making the text hard to read?

Here is an example poster layout:

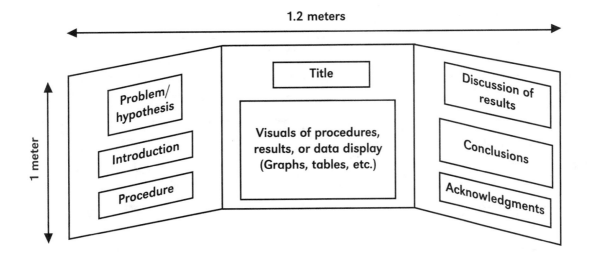

RESEARCH DESIGN PEER REVIEW FORM

Name of Reviewer _____ Date _____

Project Reviewed _____

Is the research question clearly defined?

Very clear	❑	**Comments about what was done well:**
Mostly clear	❑	
Somewhat clear	❑	**Suggestions for improvement:**
Largely unclear	❑	

Are the procedures clearly described?

Very clear	❑	**Comments about what was done well:**
Mostly clear	❑	
Somewhat clear	❑	**Suggestions for improvement:**
Largely unclear	❑	

How well do the procedures address the research question?

Very well	❑	**Comments about what was done well:**
OK	❑	
Minor problems	❑	**Suggestions for improvement:**
Needs work	❑	

RESEARCH REPORT PEER REVIEW FORM

Name of Reviewer _____ **Date** _____

Project Reviewed _____

After reading an invasive species research report written by other students, answer the following questions. Remember to keep your answers friendly and constructive.

1. What was a particular strength in this research design?

2. Do you agree with the conclusions? Do they appear to be supported by the results of the research?

3. What suggestions can you make for improving this research or report?

POSTER PEER REVIEW FORM

Name of Reviewer _____ Date _____

Project Reviewed _____

KEY
1—Largely unclear
2—Somewhat clear
3—Mostly clear
4—Very clear

	(−)		(+)
Does the poster include: Title, Research Question, Hypothesis, Procedure, Results, Conclusions, and Acknowledgments?	1	2	3	4
Is there a clear statement of the research question and hypothesis?	1	2	3	4
Does the experiment appear to be designed appropriately to address the research question?	1	2	3	4
Are the procedures described in enough detail for the experiment to be copied by someone else?	1	2	3	4
Are the data presented clearly?	1	2	3	4
Is there a clear explanation of the results?	1	2	3	4
Do the conclusions seem well supported by the data?	1	2	3	4
Were the presenters able to answer questions clearly?	1	2	3	4
Is the poster attractive and easy to read and understand?	1	2	3	4

TOTAL SCORE _____

COMMENTS:
What was a particular strength of this research design?

What suggestions do you have for improving either this research or the poster presentation?